Arab Indianapolis

Printed in the United States of America
First edition 2022
1 2 3 4 5 6 7 8 9

ISBN: 978-1-953368-27-0

Belt Publishing
5322 Fleet Avenue
Cleveland, Ohio 44105
www.beltpublishing.com

Cover art by David Wilson
Book design by David Wilson

Arab Indianapolis

Edward E. Curtis IV

CONTENTS

CIRCLE TOWER

The history of Arab Americans in Indianapolis is largely unknown, but they have helped to shape the life of Indianapolis's best-known places, including the heart of downtown. *Credit: Edward Curtis.*

MEZZA
CHEESE SAMPLER
SALAD
WATERMELON
SOFT DRINKS
BOTTLED WATER
GRAPE LEAVES
SPANAKOPITA

The annual Middle East festival at St. George Antiochian Orthodox Church celebrates the heritage of the church's Arabic-speaking founders from Syria and Lebanon. *Credit: Vinnie Manganello.*

CHRONOLOGY

1900: At least 208 Arabic-speaking immigrants live in Indiana; Sadie Hider is one of them.

1905: Martha and Salma Freije arrive in the Syrian colony on Willard Street.

1910: Syrian immigrants in Indiana total more than one thousand people.

1917: Arab Hoosiers serve in World War I, and some gain US citizenship.

1924: The National Origins Act virtually bans immigration from Syria; Julia David weds Nicholas Shaheen.

1926: St. George Syrian Orthodox Church opens.

1927: Waheeb Salim Zarick receives MD degree from Indiana University.

1935: Dozens of Arabic-speaking grocers operate in Indianapolis.

1936: The Syrian American Brotherhood clubhouse hosts the first meeting of the Midwest Federation of Syrian and Lebanese Clubs.

1937: John Haramy finishes his dissertation at Indiana University, *The Palestine Mandate: A Study in Conflicting Interests.*

1944: Corporal Mitchell Tamer is killed in the Allied campaign to defeat Nazi Germany.

1957: Michael Tamer leads fundraising for St. Jude Children's Hospital.

1964: Helen Corey becomes the first Arab American elected to statewide office.

1965: The Immigration and Naturalization Act opens the door to more Arab immigrants.

1972: St. Vincent's Hospital asks Dr. William Nasser to establish its cardiology center.

1990: Former Warren Central High School quarterback Jeff George is selected first overall in NFL draft by the Indianapolis Colts.

2004: Mitch Daniels, grandson of Syrian immigrants, is elected Indiana governor.

2010: The US Census reports 19,720 Hoosiers of Arab descent; the Arab American Institute says it's 46,122.

2015: Governor Mike Pence attempts, unsuccessfully, to ban Syrian refugees from settling in Indiana.

2017: Immigrants to Indianapolis from Egypt, Iraq, and Jordan increase; Syrians and Lebanese remain the largest group.

2018: Nermeen Mouftah, a specialist in Islamic studies, is appointed assistant professor at Butler University.

2020: Fady Qaddoura is the first Arab Muslim elected to the Indiana State Senate.

INTRODUCTION

Arabic-speaking people began settling in Indianapolis in the late 1800s. Coming mainly from what are today the countries of Syria and Lebanon but was then part of the Ottoman Empire, these immigrants were people of modest means who arrived in the United States in search of economic opportunity. Life in the eastern Mediterranean, as in most of the world, was changing. Even as the global economy expanded, many people were actually worse off as their traditional ways of making a living disappeared. During the same period, America was in need of cheap labor, and it encouraged mass immigration. As a result, more than a million immigrants from Eastern and Southern Europe and the Ottoman Empire came to the United States in the late nineteenth and early twentieth centuries.

Tens of thousands of them were Arabic speakers. By 1910, there were about one thousand people of Arab descent in Indianapolis. Some worked in area factories, while others—especially those who lived in the Syrian quarter on Willard Street—made their living as peddlers. By World War I, the Syrians of Indianapolis also established successful businesses, including grocery stores and retail shops. Their male and female children—sometimes born in Syria, sometimes born in America—attended public schools and sometimes college or university. Some followed in their parents' footsteps as entrepreneurs; others became professionals and nonprofit leaders in Indianapolis. Many served in World War I.

Alice Carter's Orthodox Christian grandparents were among the Arabic-speaking pioneers who settled in Indianapolis. *Credit: St. George Church.*

Despite their decades-long presence in America, there was strong anti-immigrant feeling in the country, and the 1924 National Origins Act virtually banned immigration from Syria and other parts of Asia. It would not be until after World War II that significant numbers of Arab people would once again come to the United States. In the 1950s, students from North Africa and the Middle East began to study in Indiana's colleges and universities. After 1965, when the United States reformed its racist immigration system, more and more Arabs, especially health care professionals, scientists, and engineers, settled in the area. These Arabs, both Christians and Muslims, immigrated for what they saw as the unprecedented economic opportunity as well as the freedom to practice their religion without government interference.

Some Arab immigrants, especially political exiles and refugees, also came to the United States in order to escape repression or violence in their homelands. Events such as the 1967 Arab-Israeli war, the 1975 Lebanese civil war, the 1991 Somali civil war, the 1992 military coup in Algeria, the US invasion of Iraq in 2003, and the 2011 Syrian civil war resulted in an increase in the Arabic-speaking population of Indianapolis.

In 2017, the US Census Bureau estimated that there were 28,314 Hoosiers of Arab descent. Marion County was home to 5,688 Arab Americans, while 3,197 lived in Hamilton County. These two central Indiana counties accounted for almost a third of all Arab Hoosiers. People who traced their ancestry to Lebanon remained the largest single group of Arab Americans in the state. But between 2009 and 2016, there were significant increases in the number of immigrants from Egypt, Iraq, Jordan, Morocco, and Yemen. According to the Arab American Institute, these numbers from the US Census Bureau likely underestimate the number of Arab-descended people in Arab Indianapolis.

Whatever the precise number of Arab Americans living in Greater Indianapolis, they have made a remarkable impact. From establishing businesses to working in the fields of health care and education, they have contributed to the

Samia Alajlouni, who immigrated to the United States from Jordan in 2003, has served as coordinator of a mental health program for displaced Syrians in Jordan, as communication specialist in the Community Health Engagement Program of the Indiana Clinical and Translational Sciences Institute, and as secretary of the Indiana Muslim Advocacy Network. *Credit: Ziad Hefni.*

cultural vitality, economic growth, and social fabric of central Indiana. *Arab Indianapolis* unearths the lost and surprising history of this community. This book features the stories of Arab Americans who are well-known and those who are not. It reveals a history hidden in plain sight, sometimes buried underneath Indianapolis's most iconic landmarks such as Lucas Oil Stadium, Monument Circle, the Indiana War Memorials, the Indiana Capitol, the Governor's Residence, and Riverside Park. It also features compelling profiles of and interviews with contemporary Arab Hoosiers. Written in an accessible style, this book depicts Arab Indianapolis as much through images as through words, allowing you to understand in a tangible way the lives of Arab-descended Hoosiers who call Indianapolis their home.

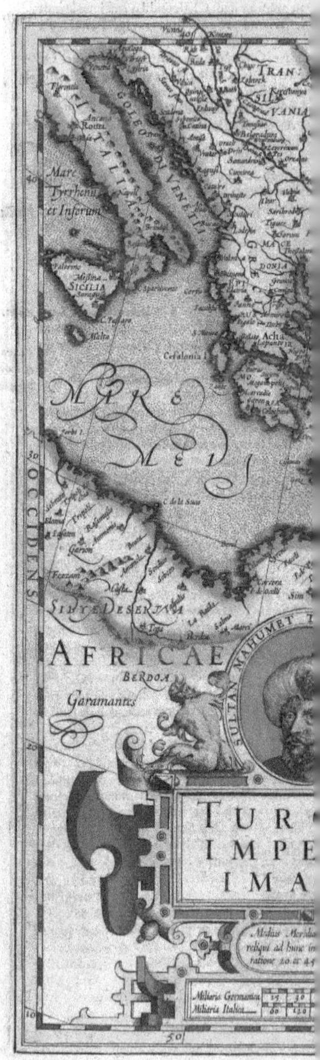

Who Is Arab?

Let's start with a simple answer. If people call themselves Arab, then generally speaking, we should take their word for it.

Today, the people who refer to themselves as Arabs live mainly in North Africa and West Asia (also called the Middle East). The Arab world includes the countries or territories of Mauritania, Western Sahara, Morocco, Algeria, Tunisia, Libya, Egypt, Sudan, Djibouti, Somalia, Palestine, Lebanon, Syria, Jordan, Saudi Arabia, Yemen, Oman, United Arab Emirates, Bahrain, Qatar, Kuwait, and Iraq.

As of 2019, the World Bank estimated that the total population of Arabs was 428 million. Arabs also live in other parts of the world, including the United States, where 2 to 3.7 million people claim Arab ancestry.

But what else makes an Arab person "Arab"?

It's not race. Arabs can be white, brown, or Black.

Before the twentieth century, most Arabic-speaking people lived under the authority of the Ottoman Empire, whose boundaries are depicted in this 1606 map by J. Hondius. *Credit: Wiki Commons.*

It's also not religion. The majority of Arabs are Muslim, but there are also Arabic-speaking Christians and Jews, as well as other religious minorities and people without any religious affiliation in the Arab world. In the United States, Arab American Christians may be more numerous than Arab American Muslims.

Today, the term "Arab" is much more akin to the label of "Latinx" or "Hispanic." It is often used by Arab people to say that they share a common heritage that is tied, one way or another, to the Arabic language.

People called Arabs lived in ancient Syria and Arabia hundreds of years before the Common Era. An early myth of their origins is that they were the children of Ishmael. Their language was spoken by a relatively small number of people until Muslim political authority extended beyond the Arabian Peninsula. During the Middle Ages, Arabic became the predominant language of traders, scientists, philosophers, lawyers, scholars, poets, religious teachers, and mystics across North Africa, the Middle East, and parts of Europe, including Spain and Sicily.

In the late 1800s and early 1900s, the term "Arab" took on a different meaning as it became associated with the political movement to establish independent nation-states in North Africa and the Middle East. The idea that people shared a common heritage was a powerful way to bridge or even repress various differences under a common national banner.

In the United States, the term "Arab American" has a history tied for many to political empowerment and cultural pride. Before World War I, most Arab Americans in Indianapolis traced their roots to Syria, which then included the countries of Syria, Lebanon, Palestine, and Jordan. After World War II, the number of Arabic-speaking people from other countries increased. In the late 1960s and early 1970s, the term "Arab American" became increasingly popular as an ethnic label.

Arab Indianapolis explores this history in an intimate way, highlighting the rich diversity and contributions of the Arab American community since the late 1800s. We celebrate our Arab American heritage without apology while also being sensitive to the diversity, and even the shortcomings, of our community. In other words, we embrace our full humanity.

CHAPTER ONE
FROM PEDDLERS TO GROCERY STORE OWNERS

In the late 1800s, the first Arabic-speaking residents of Indianapolis initially came to the public's attention as peddlers. In truth, many Arab Americans in Indianapolis also worked in the city's factories and performed other kinds of generally unskilled labor. But peddling was one of the foundations of Arab Indianapolis, and many of those peddlers went on to become successful dry goods and grocery store owners.

Willard Street: Indianapolis's Syrian Colony

> Joy supreme has reigned in the Syrian colony on Willard Street since 3 o'clock on Wednesday morning when David Freije hugged to his breast for the first time in eight years his wife Martha and their seven-year-old daughter Salomey, whom he had never seen before.
>
> —*Indianapolis Morning Star*, 1905

It took all of grocer David Freije's hard-earned $400 in savings, the equivalent of over $10,000 in today's dollars, to bring his wife Martha and young daughter, Salomey, from Ottoman Syria.

They made their first home in America on Willard Street, located on a piece of land currently occupied by Lucas Oil Stadium, the home of the Indianapolis Colts National Football League team. Long before the Colts came to Indianapolis from Baltimore, Arabic-speaking immigrants lived on a road that was about as long as football field. It ran over Pogue's Run creek between Senate and Capitol Streets. The *Indianapolis Journal* described Willard Street as a "short thoroughfare divided into two parts by a dirty little stream whose banks in this particular vicinity were laden with tin cans, old shoes and other rubbish."

According to the US Census, in 1910, David S. Freije (1874–1955), his spouse Martha (1876–1958), and Salomey were living at 524 Willard, and their family had grown to include two-year-old Eddie and a baby, Mary. Joseph Freije, twenty-six, boarded with them and was part-owner of the store.

They were not the only people named Freije who lived on Willard Street. David T. Freije (1846–1931) and Sadie Freije (1857–1944) lived at 502

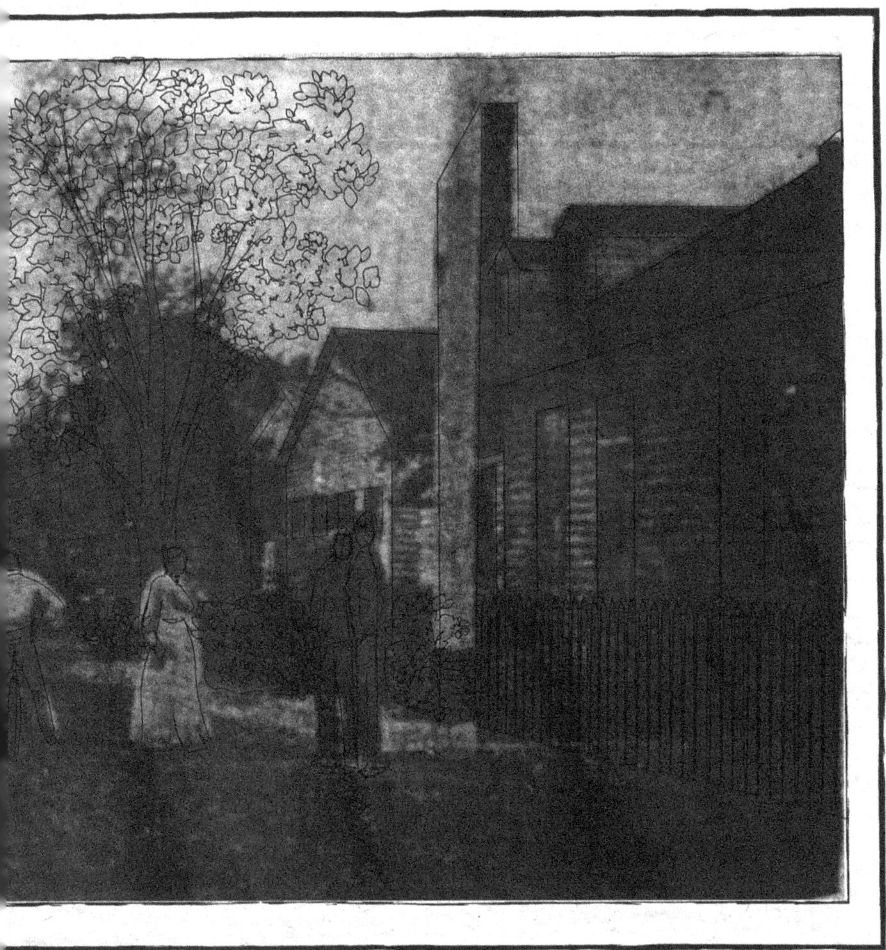

This photograph of Willard Street from 1906, enhanced by illustrator Jessica Dunn, appeared in the *Indianapolis News* as part of an article that extolled the cosmopolitan nature of immigrant communities in the city.

Willard. Charles Freije and Mary Freije, who was the widow of Abraham, had households there as well.

Even though a 1902 *Indianapolis Journal* article labeled Willard Street the city's "Syrian Colony," Arab Americans were actually a minority of its total residents. According to a December 26, 1903, *Indianapolis Star* article, the street's narrow, wood-framed houses were also inhabited by African Americans, Italians, Poles, Greeks, and Hungarians. This was a racially integrated neighborhood. Of the 179 people counted as residents of Willard Street in the 1900 US census, fifty-five were Black.

The *Journal* estimated that there were about a hundred Syrians on the street, but the 1900 US census only counted twenty-seven. It is difficult to know which number is correct. The majority of Syrian men on Willard Street made their living as peddlers, which means that they were gone for long stretches at a time. Some temporary residents stayed for only a short while in other people's houses—perhaps up to ten people would lodge in these small abodes—before moving on or finding a place of their own. Other Syrians preferred not to reveal their identities to others, including census employees, because they feared it would only stoke the racial and ethnic discrimination that they faced. Though the US census listed Syrians as "white," the *Journal* called them "Orientals." It would take a couple decades before the city's opinion makers would think of most Syrian and Lebanese people as white.

Some Arab families translated their names to English or simply took different names; this was a typical practice among many immigrants at the time. Among those listed as having been born in Syria were George and Mary Forest, Jacob and Annie Joseph, and David and Sadie Rogers.

The *Journal* said that the Syrian colony began in the 1890s, when Arabic speakers immigrated to Indianapolis from Rablah, a town which was then part of the Ottoman Empire but today is located in central Syria, just across the northeast border of Lebanon.

Syrian women were vital to the success of the neighborhood. In 1900, there were at least three female heads of household. If you visited during the week, said the *Indianapolis Journal*, you would find women rising early and working late. Since most of the men were out peddling, often far away from Indianapolis, it was the women who gathered scraps from a nearby lumberyard to fuel their stoves. "Their daily work is quite enough to dispel all preconceived ideas regarding the indolence and helplessness of Oriental women," wrote the *Journal*. The writer couldn't believe that such small women could carry such large loads of lumber.

On Sunday, the men of the colony, back from their peddling, would sit in front of their houses. The residents would dress in their finest clothes. Mutton would be cooked and shared with all. The *Journal* thought that the residents were participating in "some kind of joyous Mohammedan celebration," but most of the people on the street likely belonged to Orthodox or other Arab Christian communities. Many of them celebrated Christmas and Easter at different times than Western Christians, and their Arab feasting traditions were likely mistaken as Muslim by the reporter.

Sadie Hider: A Founding Mother of Arab Indianapolis

In 1900, Syrian immigrant Sadie Hider, the daughter of Elias and Janicy Freije, was listed in the US census as the head of her household, responsible for taking care of her three kids. She was married to John (or Hanna) Hider, but it's not clear where her husband was at the time. Maybe he returned to Ottoman Syria for a while. Maybe he was just gone the day that the census was taken. Sadie could not speak, read, or write English, so it is possible that there was a miscommunication.

Sadie Hider's house was located north of Pogue's Run and a factory that later housed the Wizard Auto Company.

Mrs. Hider lived at 528 Willard. She inhabited one half of a wood-framed duplex, which was one and a half stories high. It was a "shotgun house," only about fifteen feet wide. The roof was made of wood shingles.

Her life on Willard Street must not have been easy. Just a few years after the 1900 census, Sadie's son, Tom, died and was buried in Holy Cross and St. Joseph Cemetery south of town.

It was fortunate that Sadie Hider had friends and relatives who lived, like she did, in the heart of Arabic-speaking Indianapolis. When the census was taken in 1910, forty-two-year-old John Hider, her husband, was listed as head of household. He may not have been the easiest man to live with. On July 2, 1911, he was arrested for assault against a man named Obla Black. According to the *Indianapolis Star*, Hider confronted the man, who was African American, and "commanded him to dance, pointing a revolver at the colored man's feet." Mr. Black "struck his hand against the revolver and was injured."

A few years later, John Hider died. But working with her two boys, Sadie Hider supported herself by operating a corner grocery store located on the 500 block of Blake Street. She also saw both of her boys get married. Her son John wed Selma Freije, another resident of Willard Street. The connections among the Freije, Hider, and Kafoure families fueled the growth of Syrian charitable, social, and religious associations in Indianapolis, including St. George Syrian Orthodox Church, where Sadie was a member.

Sadie Freije Hider may not have started out with much, but she lived long enough to see her children succeed in business and to see her grandchildren excel in Indianapolis's public schools. Her granddaughter Evelyn was an honor roll student at Washington High, where she also served as stage manager for one of the junior vaudevilles. Her grandson Robert appeared in an ethnic Christmas program at the Children's Museum, representing Syrian Americans, and he went on to play football and become a school ambassador at Washington High.

When Sadie Hider died in 1940, she was mourned not only by her immediate family members, such as her sister Mary Kafoure and her brothers, Frank and Fred Freije, but also by the whole Syrian community. Her funeral took place at St. George.

Three years later, her sons, John and Lewis, still missed her. They published a poem in the *Indianapolis Star* in her memory: "Oft we think of you, dear mother, / And our hearts are sad with pain; / Oh, this world would be heaven / Could we hear your voice again. / You wore a crown of patience / As you struggled on and on, / A faithful one, so kind and true. / Dear mother, how we long for you." It was a fitting tribute to one of the mothers of Arab Indianapolis, a woman whose perseverance had created the possibility of a thriving community.

LUCAS OIL
STADIUM

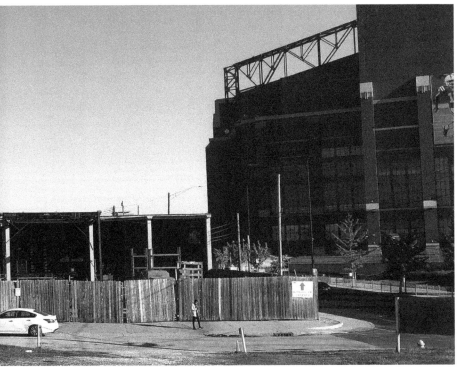

By 1910, Sadie Hider had moved a few blocks away to 401 West Norwood Street, located southwest of today's Lucas Oil Stadium. *Credit: Edward Curtis.*

The Syrian Corner Grocery

Sadie Hider was one of many grocery store owners in Arab Indianapolis. By 1915, there were at least eighteen Arabic-speaking grocers in Indianapolis—seven of them had the last name of Freije—and Arab-owned groceries were located far beyond the Syrian colony downtown.

Peddlers were natural grocers. They understood how to move merchandise and what customers wanted to buy. But just as importantly, they built the supply networks necessary to open a store with little capital. They knew people who could lend them the money and goods to stock their shelves. Once new store owners succeeded, they would help others, especially people from their family or their village.

Some Syrian groceries prided themselves on obtaining the very best produce, seeds, and other items. In 1915, for example, the Abraham Brothers, located at 728 East Vermont in Lockerbie Square, competed in multiple categories at the state fair and consistently won, placed, or showed. They got first prize for old white corn and old white flint corn; third place for golden popcorn; first for Red Fultz wheat; third for black oats; first for Timothy seed; and second for White Seneca Beauty potatoes. The winning streak continued in 1916 with quinces, White Burley tobacco, and York Imperial apples.

The corner store was not always located on an actual street corner. But it was almost always small in size. The refrigeration revolution transformed the dry goods stores of the early 1900s into true grocery stores. Frigidaire display cases replaced iceboxes. In addition to the grains, canned goods, lard, tobacco products, and notions offered by the dry goods store, groceries sold fresh meat, poultry, and milk.

Abraham and Latifa Freije, married in 1911, are pictured with their children (left to right): Corrine, Louise, John, Mabel, and Mary. Abraham was from the village of Ra'it, located in Lebanon's Bekaa Valley. Latifa was from Baskinta in the Lebanese mountains. *Credit: Chitwood Media.*

| Freije Abraham, dry

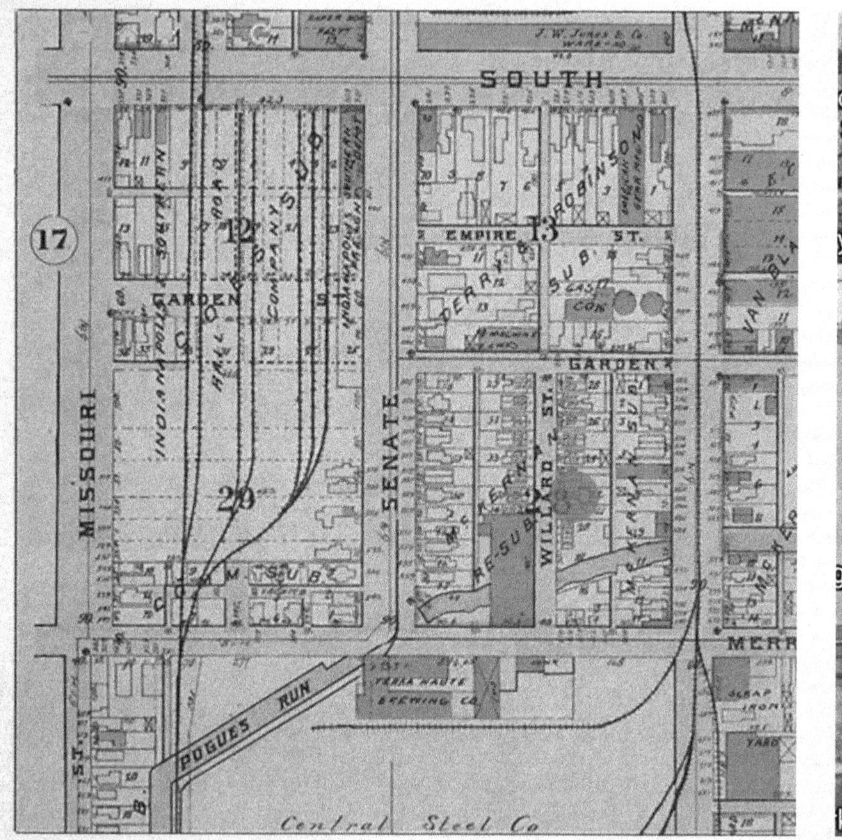

INDIANAPOLIS SYRIAN COLONY

:4 Willard.

TREET - 1915

In 1915, Abraham Freije operated a dry goods store on Willard Street in the historic heart of Arab Indianapolis. *Credit: Chitwood Media.*

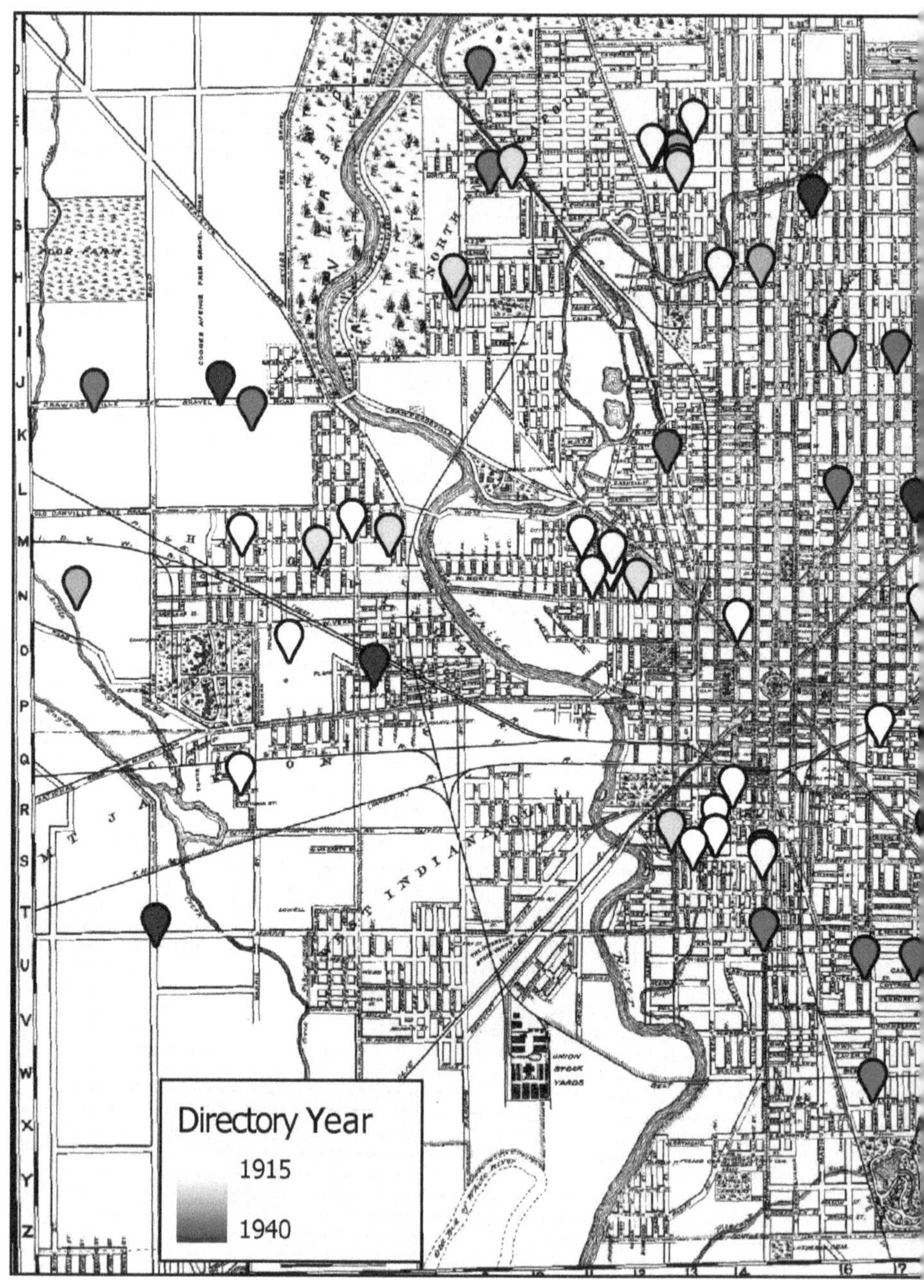

Directory Year
1915
1940
UNION STOCK YARDS

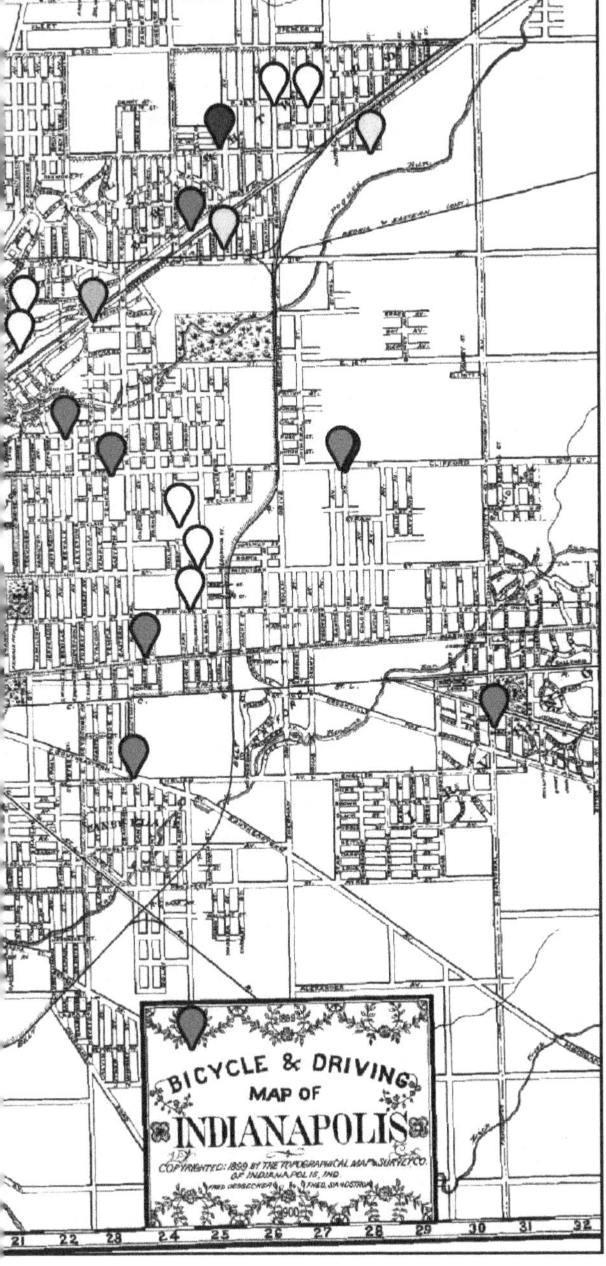

By 1915, Syrian-owned groceries were located on the east side and the west side as well as in downtown Indianapolis. By 1940, the stores could be found in every part of the city. *Credit: Jeffrey S. Wilson.*

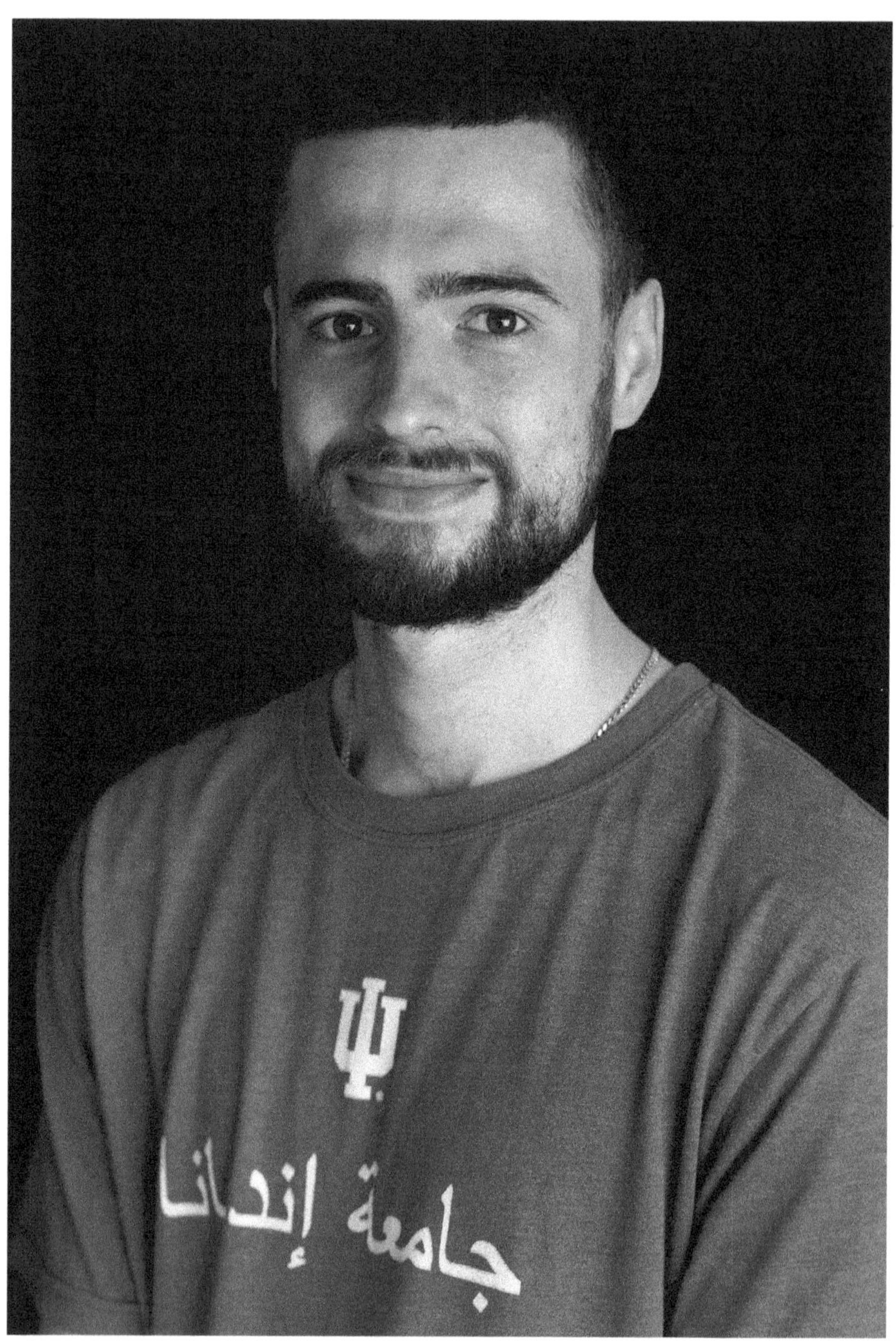

Josh Chitwood is a descendant of grocers Abraham and Latifa Freije. He has made a documentary about the search for his Syrian and Lebanese roots in Indianapolis. His T-shirt reads "Indiana University" in Arabic. *Credit: Ziad Hefni.*

Diana Najjar is a third-generation Lebanese American who taught at the Orchard School for three decades. She traces her Indianapolis roots to her grandfather, Shukrulah Saliba, who became known as John Joseph in the United States after immigrating to America in the late nineteenth century. Her son, David Najjar, is a Hamilton County Judge. *Credit: Ziad Hefni.*

Corner grocery stores also functioned as essential financial institutions. Just like today, many unbanked Americans cashed their paychecks at the stores. Even more importantly, during the Great Depression, the corner grocery helped to stave off hunger. Store owners offered temporary credit to customers. When customers got their paycheck, they would sign it over to the store, pay their bill, and buy more groceries. When customers were unemployed, the store would sometimes carry them for months at a time.

Because stores always had cash on hand, it could also be a dangerous business. Robberies were a regular part of life for many Syrian grocers, who were sometimes killed during the stickups. For instance, at 9:30 p.m. on Saturday, September 17, 1932, Sam Ajamie was working with his brother and another Syrian in his store on 1448 Roosevelt Avenue when two men came into the store and asked for fish. "Before Sam Ajamie could answer, both men drew revolvers," according to a September 19 article in the *Indianapolis Star*. The grocers all raised their hands, but one of the thieves shot Sam Ajamie anyway. "Ajamie then seized the bandit's revolver and wrested it from him," according to the police report. Ajamie chased the men out of the store and went to City Hospital for treatment, but he had been shot in the chest and did not recover. He left behind six children. Ajamie's funeral took place at St. Philip Neri Church, and he was buried at Holy Cross Cemetery.

The corner grocery business was not without its challenges, but Arab Indianapolis would not have been the same without it. By 1935, there were at least forty-three Syrian and Lebanese groceries in Indianapolis. The Corey, Freije, Haboush, Hider, and Mesalam families owned multiple stores. One woman, Mrs. Fannie Lautif, was listed as a store owner. She was a widow. Her store was located at 1947 Ludlow, on the east side of town just north of the Peerless Foundry Company, which made coal, gas, and oil furnaces.

These grocery stores were a cornerstone of Arab Indianapolis society. The money made and the know-how gained in running these stores also supported the establishment of community organizations. Indianapolis became a center of Arab American life in the 1930s at least in part because of the success of the Syrian corner grocery.

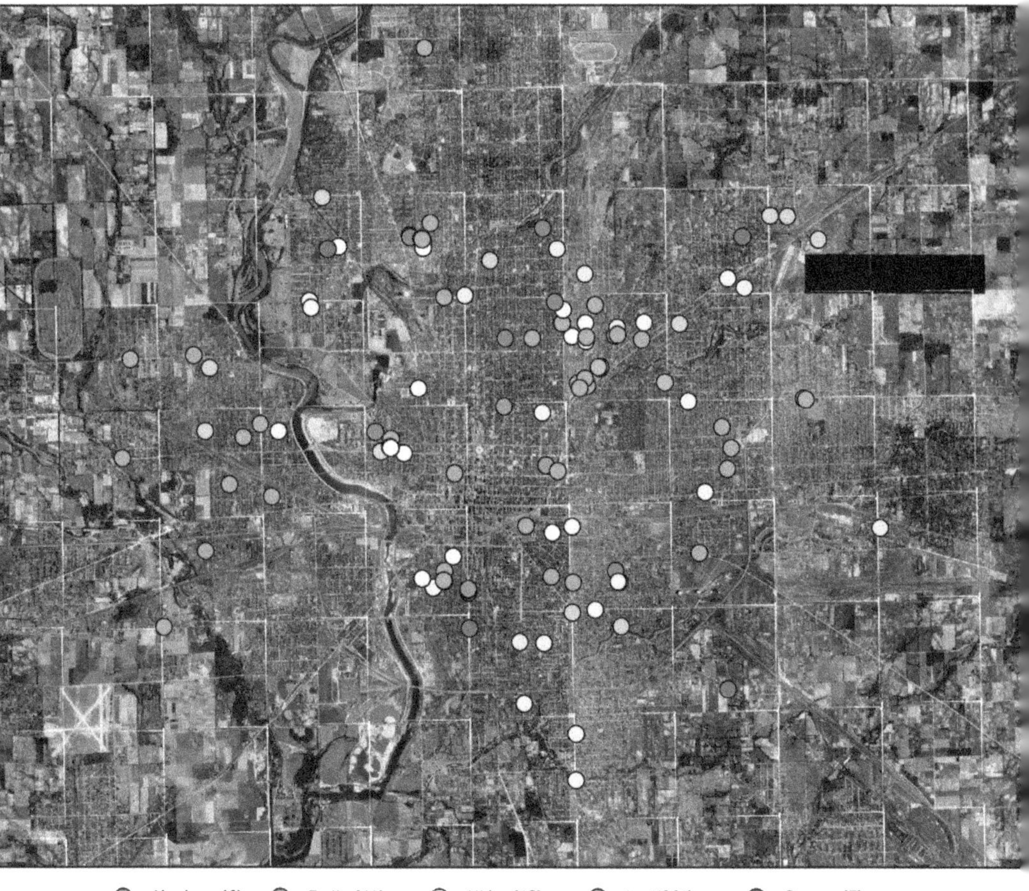

This map depicts the golden age of the Arab-owned family grocery store in Indianapolis. It shows the number of times a store owned by a Syrian family appeared in the 1915, 1920, 1930, 1935, and 1940 city directories at a given location. *Credit: Jeffrey S. Wilson.*

In 1973, Jeff George was among the Sunday School students from St. George who went to Kings Island amusement park near Cincinnati. *Credit: Norma Johns, St. George.*

PROFILE: NFL Quarterback Jeff George

Born to David George and Judith Smith George on December 8, 1967, Jeff George is perhaps the most important professional Arab American athlete in Indianapolis sports history.

In 1984 and 1985, he quarterbacked the Warren Central High School football team to consecutive state championships. His high school trophy shelf was graced by every award imaginable—national male high school athlete of the year, national football player of the year, and Nicola Award for the most outstanding football player in the nation.

He was the pride of Indianapolis, and especially of the Arab American community in which he was raised.

On his father's side, part of George's family traces its roots to the city of Saidnaya, located less than twenty miles north of Damascus, the capital of Syria. It is a mountain town about 5,000 feet above sea level. Snowy in the winter and warm in the summer, Saidnaya has been a center of Christian religious life in the Middle East for more than a thousand years. To this day, there are dozens of chapels and monasteries from various Orthodox, Catholic, and Syriac religious communities, and Christians from around the world undertake pilgrimages to this sacred site. Many venerate its ancient icon of the Virgin Mary, seeking blessings or help when they wish to conceive a child. Muslims also visit the shrine; in this part of the world, the children of Abraham have a long history of sharing religious figures and sacred sites. Despite the news headlines, there is a history in the Arab world of interreligious cooperation as well as conflict.

There was a whole group of Christians from Saidnaya and the greater Damascus area that arrived in Indiana at the beginning of the 1900s. They were among the most important figures in the establishment of St. George Syrian Orthodox Church.

Saidnaya is a site of pilgrimage for Christians and Muslims who celebrate the feast day of Mary, also called Our Lady of Saidnaya. *Credit: Wiki Commons.*

Jeff George's great-grandfather, Sam Risk Corey, was one of them. Like many other Syrian immigrants to Indianapolis, he became a grocer, operating Corey's Food Market at 2128 North Olney with his wife, Mary.

George's other Arab great-grandparents were John and Rose (Ramsa) Khalil George. They also operated a grocery store, located at 521 East Twenty-First Street in today's Kennedy King neighborhood. When they first arrived, they were sometimes known by a different last name, Ozman.

The Corey and George families came together in the marriage of their American-born children, Joe George and Ruth Corey, who were the grandparents of the future NFL quarterback. Joe was the owner of the Panda Restaurant on 12 West Ohio. Ruth, who became one of her grandson's biggest fans, frequently volunteered at St. George Church, where she starred in a revue celebrating the fiftieth anniversary of the congregation in 1982.

St. George, like many other religious congregations in Indianapolis and the United States, supported youth sports, including a successful church basketball team. Sports were not seen as a contradiction of the church's mission but as a way to keep young people involved in the life of the congregation and maybe teach some important lessons along the way. Jeff George always kept a part of his church with him, even on the field, where he wore an Orthodox cross given to him by his grandmother.

For young Jeff George, sports became a devotion. He played baseball and basketball, competing with and against his two brothers. But it was on the gridiron where he made his mark on Indianapolis history. After graduating from Warren Central, George played in college for Purdue and the University of Illinois. Then, in 1990, he was the very first person selected in the National Football League draft.

His hometown team, the Indianapolis Colts, signed him to a contract worth about $15 million,

Jeff George played in the Hoosier Dome, which was the home of the Indianapolis Colts before Lucas Oil Stadium. *Credit: Wiki Commons.*

reportedly the most money ever offered to a rookie at the time. The Colts, who played during that era at the Hoosier Dome, had a 7–9 record in George's first year, but the rookie threw for sixteen touchdowns and 2,152 yards, enough to earn him honors as the quarterback on the NFL's all-rookie team. He spent four seasons with the Colts, but they did not make the playoffs during his tenure.

In twelve seasons, Jeff George played for five NFL teams. In 1995, he led the Atlanta Falcons to the playoffs, throwing for a total of 4,143 yards during the regular season. In 1997, as a member of the Oakland Raiders, George threw more yards than any other quarterback in the league. He also tossed twenty-nine touchdown passes—the most in his career. Two years later, George began the season as the backup quarterback for the Minnesota Vikings' Randall Cunningham, but he took over as starter with ten games left in the regular season. Under George's leadership, the Vikings went 8–2, and George won his first-ever NFL playoff game.

Today, the George legacy continues. Arab Americans and others in Indianapolis watched with delight as Jeff George Jr. inherited his father's mantle. He too attended Warren Central High School and led his team to a state football championship as quarterback. He also followed in his father's footsteps by playing college football at the University of Illinois, though he subsequently transferred to the University of Pittsburgh.

The George family is one of several Arab American families who have made their mark on the history of football. Just consider this list of Arab American NFL players, coaches, and owners: Abe Gibron, Bill George, Joe Robbie, Rich Kotite, John Elway, Doug Flutie, Brian Habib, Drew Haddad, Robert Saleh, Gibran Hamdan, Ryan Kalil, Matt Kalil, and Oday Aboushi.

In the George family, Arab Indianapolis has a claim on that rich history too.

CHAPTER TWO

BUILDING INSTITUTIONS

Willard Street remained an important Arab community for two decades after the first Syrian families arrived. In 1915, some of these families were gone—some returned to Syria, others simply moved to other places in Indianapolis. There were still Freijes living there, though, and new families had arrived—the Kafoures and the Bashhours. Seven of the thirty households on Willard Street remained occupied by Arab Americans.

By 1920, however, no Arab families remained on Willard. The number of housing units available dwindled as the area was repurposed. The east side of the street was cleared away to build a railroad line, and a basket factory was added to the west side of the street. Many Arab Americans continued to live nearby, but some moved to other parts of Indianapolis.

After World War I, these men and women built the institutions that came to define Arab American life in Indianapolis: businesses, religious congregations, social clubs, and philanthropic organizations. Some of the children of peddlers and grocery store owners became professionals, especially in the health care industry. Together, they changed the history of Indianapolis.

Julia David, Nicholas Shaheen, and Monument Circle

She was a poet. He was an entrepreneur.

They both grew up in Indianapolis's Arabic-speaking Syrian community, and like many sons and daughters of immigrants in the era between World War I and World War II, when the time came to get married, they chose to wed someone from their own ethnic group.

Nicholas Shaheen dons a hatta, or headscarf; an agal, the band that holds it in place; and a cloak. *Credit: Bretzman Collection, Indianapolis Historical Society.*

NICHOLAS SHAHEEN
ORIENTAL RUGS LINENS
45

The left side of today's Hilbert Circle Theater, home of the Indianapolis Symphony Orchestra, was the storefront for the Shaheen's rug shop. *Credit: Indiana Historical Society P0767, Vinnie Manganello.*

Julia David was born in Indianapolis to Habeeb and Sadie David, both immigrants from Syria, in 1901. Habeeb, like so many early immigrants, made his living as a peddler. In 1897, he married Sadie. Two years later, in 1899, the city directory listed their residence as 536 South Capitol Avenue.

Julia David may have come from modest means, but she grew up in a family that believed in civic engagement. Her father was a Shriner, taking part in fundraising and performances at the Murat Temple. She followed his example. As a teenager, Julia David volunteered at Indianapolis's Young Women's Christian Association, where she participated in theatrical productions and raised money for mission trips and sympathy banks.

After graduating from high school, Julia David attended DePauw University in Greencastle, Indiana. Although a minority of Americans still attended college by the time Julia David became a student, the number of women who entered higher education increased dramatically after World War I. At DePauw, they were aided by a $2.5 million scholarship fund established in 1919. As a student, Julia David joined a writing and literary society called Tusitala. Some described it as a group for people who liked to write things.

While Julia David was at DePauw, her future husband was working in his family's import business. Nicholas Shaheen was born in 1901 in a small town in southern Syria called Qatana (also spelled Kattana). In 1908, Shaheen and his family left Syria and first settled in Canton, Ohio. Then, in 1912, they came to Indianapolis, where Shaheen's family sold clothing, linens, and other merchandise.

After marrying, the couple moved into the David family home at 2249 North Delaware Street. They started a family and had three daughters: Adele in 1925, Joan in 1927, and Margaret in 1930.

Nicholas Shaheen's business was growing. Originally located on 2204 North Meridian Street, near today's IU Methodist Hospital, his store offered oriental rugs, laces, and linens. In 1929, he moved the shop to the heart of Indianapolis—45 Monument Circle.

This "House of Quality," as he advertised it, claimed prominent public space in the city not just for him, but for all Syrian immigrants. Today, the entrance and box office of Hilbert Circle Theater, home of the Indianapolis Symphony Orchestra, occupies the site of the Shaheen Oriental Rug shop.

Nicholas Shaheen saw his ethnic identity as an asset. He dressed in an Arab costume more associated with desert Bedouins than urban Syrian merchants for a formal portrait taken by famed Indy 500 and *Indianapolis Star* photographer Charles Bretzman. This was no impediment to social inclusion—it was a passport. The *Star* published a number of social columns about him and his family, including a report about a visit to the Greater Hotel Gibson, described as the finest and most expensive hotel in all of Cincinnati.

Like their mother, the Shaheen daughters attended college. Joan, an honors student in high school, went to Northwestern. Adele matriculated at her mother's alma mater, DePauw, and became engaged to Richard Freije, another member of Indianapolis's Syrian community.

The story of Julia David and Nicholas Shaheen shows how, just one generation after Arabic-speaking immigrants from the Middle East arrived in Indianapolis, Hoosiers of Arab descent became prominent in the city's economic and public life. It is also a testament to the commitment of Arab immigrants to the education of their daughters. The Syrian community in Indianapolis was built through the efforts and intelligence of both men and women.

Norma Johns's family were among the founders of St. George Church. *Credit: Norma Johns, St. George Church.*

ST GEORGE
SYRIAN ORTHODOX CHURC

The Founding of St. George Syrian Church

The goal was "Easter service in the first and only Syrian church in the city." But it would not be easy. In 1925, the Syrian Christian community needed to raise $15,000 to build their own Orthodox church. That's the equivalent of hundreds of thousands of dollars today.

So these first-generation Arabic-speaking immigrants and their American-born children got to work. The women of the congregation organized a tag day. They "wore white ribbons marked Syrian orthodox church," according to the *Indianapolis Star*, "and armed with tiny American flags," they solicited donations around downtown Indianapolis.

The Knights of St. George, the Syrian Christian group in charge of the campaign, asked Hoosiers to support their efforts by signing a petition and contributing to the cause.

The first to do so was Indiana Governor Edward Jackson. Like many Hoosier politicians in the 1920s, Jackson was closely associated with the Ku Klux Klan (KKK), a white nationalist group that discriminated against and committed acts of violence against Black people as well as Catholics and Jews—in short, anyone who was not white and Protestant. Jackson secretly peddled bribes on behalf of the KKK and coveted their political muscle. In public, however, Jackson sometimes tried to reassure racial and religious minorities that he was not prejudiced against them.

By the 1920s, Syrians were increasingly accepted as white people in Indiana, but their Orthodox religion and federal policies restricting immigration from their homeland still set them apart from the white Christian establishment. Jackson's explicit endorsement of their effort to build a church was part of his broader attempt to support equality—at least in name—and expand the Republican Party's base.

Previous page: The First St. George Syrian Orthodox Church. *Credit: George Freije, St. George Church.*

Right: These steps are located at the entrance of what used to be St. George Church. The St. George lodge, built out of brick in 1934, still stands at the back of the property. *Credit: Edward Curtis.*

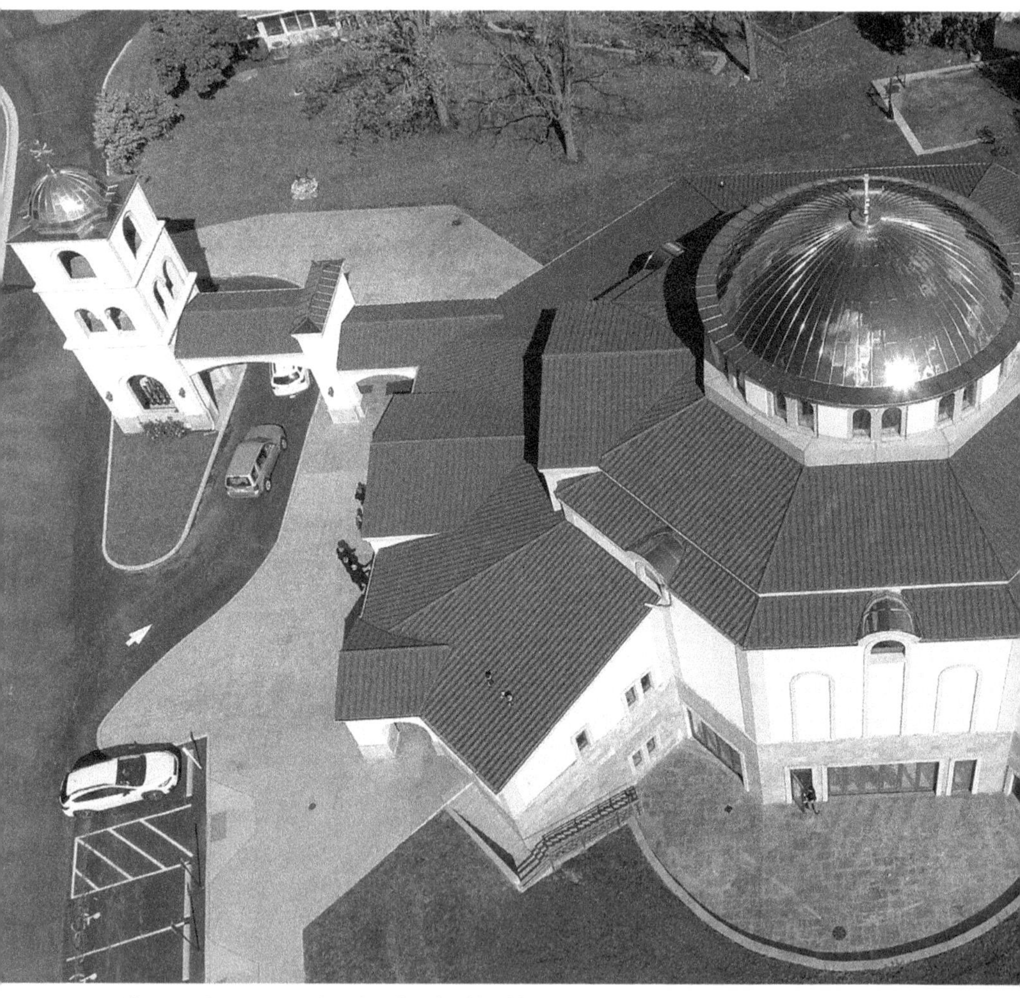

The new St. George, the church's third building, is located in Fishers, Indiana. *Credit: Vinnie Manganello.*

And it worked. In May 1926, the Knights of St. George endorsed two Republicans for the US Senate. One of them, James Watson, would go on to serve as US Senate majority leader in the era of Herbert Hoover. The Knights also publicly supported Republicans to serve as representatives in the US House, as Marion County recorder, and as Center Township Assessor.

That same year was a particularly important one for the growth and expansion of religious congregations in the city. Over a million dollars was spent on building and renovating religious congregations, including Carrollton Avenue Reformed, Fairview Presbyterian, Fountain Square Disciples of Christ, Greater St. John Baptist, and St. George: "The dedication of the St. George Syrian Orthodox church at the corner of Twenty-eighth Street and Sherman Drive," according to the *Star* on December 31, 1926, "awaits the arrival of the church officials."

By establishing their own congregation, Syrians sought not only to preserve their religious traditions but also to participate in the philanthropic, economic, and social life of Indianapolis. Religious congregations have been Americans' most popular voluntary associations, and in addition to conducting religious services, they have functioned as social and business networks, educational institutions, missionary groups, and charities. At the same time that Syrians were raising money for their church building, for example, they were also soliciting funds to aid Syrian Christians who were victims of the battle for independence in French-occupied Syria and Lebanon.

In May 1926, the Indianapolis Church Federation and Republican Mayor John Duvall endorsed this relief campaign. Duvall proclaimed, "The natives of Syria who have become citizens of our city and are interest[ed] themselves in the welfare

The interior of the new St. George Church.
Credit: Vinnie Manganello.

of the people of their native villages are worthy of our consideration." In November, national relief leader A. G. Cory of Indianapolis arranged for Archimandrite Anthony Bashir to address an open meeting at Holy Innocents Church. Speaking in colloquial Arabic and English, he hoped to inspire charitable giving among Syrians and non-Syrians alike.

In April 1927, the community's new religious congregation was officially incorporated as St. George Syrian Antiochian Church Indianapolis. The "Antiochian" refers to the original church at Antioch, the branch of Orthodox Christianity whose headquarters have been located in Damascus, Syria, since the Middle Ages.

The new church was located in the Brightwood neighborhood near the intersection of North Sherman Drive and Twenty-Eighth Street. Surrounded by a few brick buildings and wood-framed homes, it was just two and a half blocks north of the Cleveland, Cincinnati, Chicago, and St. Louis Railroad repair shops.

In June 1935, the church built a clubhouse for the Knights of St. George just behind the church. Indianapolis Mayor John W. Kern spoke at the dedication ceremony. The 750 people in attendance also enjoyed an "oriental" or Arab dinner at 1:00 p.m.

Things have changed a great deal for the church since then. Its third building, a multimillion-dollar Byzantine structure featuring a large gold dome and colorful icons, is now located in Fishers, Indiana, a suburb of Indianapolis. It is nothing like the modest brick church that once stood in Brightwood. The congregation is also more ethnically diverse. But St. George still celebrates the heritage of its founders. Its annual Middle East festival cooks up Levantine food and invites guests to dance the dabke the way its founders once did—a fitting celebration of the hard work it took to create the city's first Syrian church.

ST. GEORGE

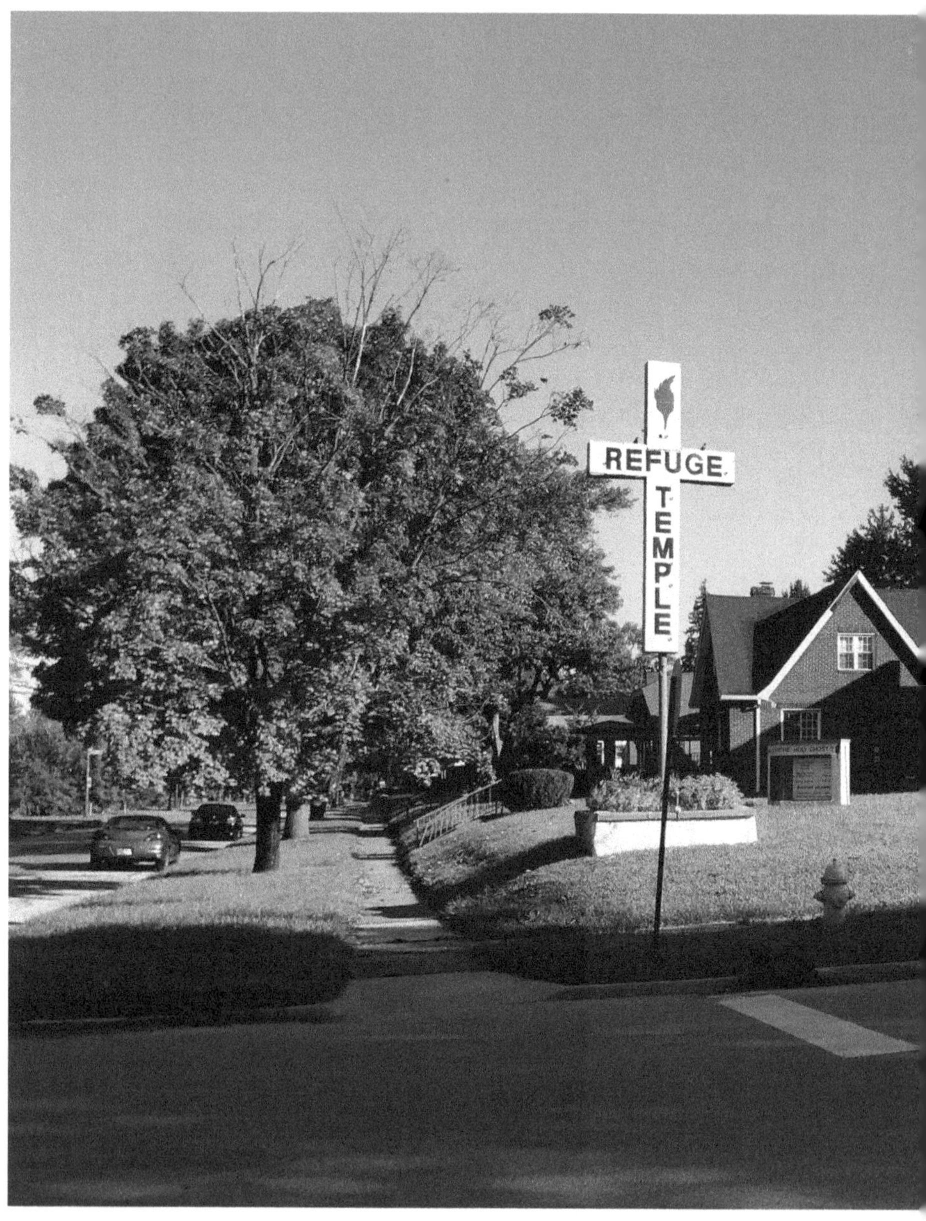

Previous page: This photograph was likely taken in the early 1960s. *Credit: Joe Shaheen, St. George Church.*

The building that once housed the social and philanthropic center of Arab Indianapolis, the Syrian American Brotherhood, was originally built as a church and became a church again after the club ceased operations there. *Credit: Edward Curtis.*

The Syrian American Brotherhood

Looking at the building today, you would have no idea how important the place used to be to Arab Indianapolis. It was a center of Arab American social and civic activities in Indianapolis, a place where some of the most important community meetings and parties of the 1930s were held.

The club had been established perhaps as early as 1919. It had rented various properties and held events in outdoor venues, but in 1930, the Syrian American Brotherhood set out to raise money for their own building. That year, they held an all-day picnic somewhere in a grove around Michigan and Kessler Boulevard. Three hundred people, including Syrians from across the state, attended the event, which featured "a three-legged race, a watermelon eating contest and an ice-holding contest." In 1931, another fundraiser was held at Crow's Nest, likely referring to the exclusive fief that was home to Eli Lilly, among other Indianapolis elites. In addition to selling food, the club organized athletic competitions, games, and a bazaar.

By the mid-1930s, the Syrian American Brotherhood purchased the former Temple Baptist Church at 2245 East Riverside. Located in a beautiful spot across the street from Riverside Park, the building looked out on the park's South Grove Golf Course, one of three different courses developed on the huge 953-acre property.

Riverside Park stretched along the White River from Eighteenth to Thirty-Eighth Street. To this day, it is still larger than New York's Central Park. It was home to a popular amusement park. Before World War II, it also featured attractive, well-kept, Spanish Mission-style architecture, a zoological department, baseball fields, bicycle and pedestrian paths, and tennis courts. Visitors paddled canoes and rowboats that were stored in the park's elegant and long boathouse on the river.

The Syrian American Brotherhood's purchase of a building on the park signaled the rise of Syrian and Lebanese immigrants and their children in the city's racial hierarchy. Black people were not welcome at Riverside Park. The city refused to issue event permits to African American groups, and the privately run amusement park explicitly barred their entry. The fact that Syrians and Lebanese operated their clubhouse in this part of town showed that this group of Arab Americans had achieved social acceptance, or at least toleration, in a white-dominated city.

The Syrian American Brotherhood hall also played a significant role in the history of Arab America when, in 1936, it hosted the organizing conference for the Midwest Federation of Syrian and Lebanese Clubs. Hundreds of

Riverside Park was a beautiful, popular, and racially segregated park in the first half of the 1900s. *Credit: Tichnor Brothers Collection, Digital Commonwealth.*

club members from Illinois, Iowa, Kansas, Kentucky, Michigan, Minnesota, Missouri, Nebraska, Ohio, and Wisconsin came at the beginning of August to organize the federation, tour the Indianapolis War Memorial, and enjoy each other's company. All the events occurred at the club. Mayor John Kern was invited to address the delegates at a grand banquet where the entertainment included Arab music and dancing. Waheeb S. Zarick was chosen as head of the federation.

It was also a place where Arab Americans had a lot of fun. The Syrian American Brotherhood was one of many social and civic organizations that enlivened the social scene in Indianapolis during the Great Depression. In 1938, the hall joined seven other venues in Indianapolis to host a benefit celebrating the birthday of President Roosevelt. The funds raised went to Riley Hospital and City Hospital, among other charities. So many Arab and non-Arab performers appeared there during this decade: Julia Taweel, a professional dancer inspired by Arab folk dancing; Dick Jurard and his orchestra; the Rosalyn Dancers; and the High Hat Orchestra.

The Syrian American Brotherhood allowed other Arab American groups to use the space for their events too. In 1936, for example, the Syrian Crescent Club staged a 9:00 p.m. dance at the clubhouse. Music was provided by the

Columbia Melodians. The next year, the same organization teamed up with the Syrian Young Men's Club to host a benefit for the Red Cross. In 1939, the Syrian So-Fra (Sorority-Fraternity) Club held a dinner and dance marking its second anniversary. Binnette L'Yome (Women of Today) also joined the So-Fra to sponsor a Speedway Hop.

In the spring of 1939, the Syrian American Brotherhood celebrated its twentieth anniversary. Habib Farrah, the "Indianapolis Syrian poet," planned to give "a history of the Brotherhood in Arabic poetry." It is remarkable that he could look back on two decades of history for this one club.

By 1939, the history of Arab Americans in Indianapolis was already more than two generations old. The first and second generations had found a lot of economic and social success in the Circle City. In spite of anti-immigrant policies that discriminated against people from Syria and Lebanon, and in spite of cultural and religious prejudices, Arab Americans did not hide their heritage. They bought a building in a prominent spot for all to see. They danced their Arab dances, served their "oriental" food to guests, and recited their Arabic poetry. Their path to integration into white America was to insist on the public recognition and respect of their ethnic identity.

Ann Zarick and Women's Leadership

Ann Kurker Zarick was ready when she received the call to become a leader in Indianapolis's Arab American community.

Born in 1897 to Jabren and Sophia Kurker, both of whom had immigrated from Syria, Ann was raised in an Arabic-speaking household. Her father was a carpenter, and hard work was a family value. Ann trained to be a stenographer. In 1918, she worked at Kahn Tailoring Company, which made uniforms

1362
1362
1362½

Previous page: Ann and Waheeb Zarick made their home south of Brookside Park on the east side of the city. *Credit: Ziad Hefni.*

Above: In 1918, Ann Kurker Zarick was working at Kahn Tailoring Company, located on 800 North Capitol. *Credit: Wiki Commons.*

for the American Expeditionary Forces in World War I. Kurker was one of 917 employees who donated to the war chest, which provided aid to members of the military, their families, and wartime refugees.

In 1926, Ann Kurker married Waheeb S. Zarick, who had almost finished his degree in medicine at Indiana University. The couple settled at 1362 North Ewing in a modest, two-story, wood-framed house just south of Brookside Park on the city's east side. Ann gave birth to her son Joseph in 1928.

Like many Syrian and Lebanese women in Indianapolis, Ann Zarick performed a lot of community service. In 1932, for example, she served on the Woman's Auxiliary for the Indianapolis Medical Society. In 1934, she was in charge of publicity for the Brookside Mothers Club, which ran activities such as children's Valentine's Day parties. Using her connections to the Indiana Society of Magicians, of which her husband served as president, she also organized a magic show for the kindergartners. All proceeds benefited the Indianapolis Free Kindergarten fund.

Ann Zarick lived in a world that was not only segregated by race but also by gender. Separate social clubs and religious groups for women were the norm. In these female spaces, women often determined the rules by which they governed themselves. They competed with one another for power, but they also enjoyed each other's company and had fun without worrying constantly about the male gaze or male chauvinism.

These groups gave women the opportunity to develop leadership skills that could also be used in mixed-gender settings. This is what happened to Ann Zarick, when in 1939, after her husband passed away prematurely, she stepped into a major leadership role in the Arab American community. That year, Mrs. Zarick led a delegation of at least nineteen Arab American men and women from Indianapolis to the annual meeting of the Midwest Federation of Syrian and Lebanese Clubs in Omaha, Nebraska. During the meeting, she was elected secretary of the regional organization.

In 1940, she once again led Indianapolis's delegation to the Midwest Federation's annual convention, held this time at the Pere Marquette in Peoria, Illinois. Three thousand delegates were expected at the meeting, where discussions were held on the formation of a national federation of Syrian and Lebanese clubs.

Ann Zarick was a respected figure in the Indianapolis community. For example, in 1939, she was one of the featured speakers at the Syrian So-Fra Club's annual dinner, which was attended by out-of-town VIPs. The next year, when the Syrian So-Fra Club installed its new leaders at the Hunters Lodge in the Marott Hotel, she was the only honored guest mentioned in the *Indianapolis News*.

Mrs. Zarick also advised the Wits Sub-Debs and Squires Club that was established in 1946. The label "sub-debs" was an abbreviation of subdebutantes,

The Marott Hotel was a premier venue for Indianapolis's white society gatherings in the 1920s and 1930s; it was the favorite spot of world-famous celebrities and dignitaries who dined or lodged there during visits to Indianapolis. *Credit: Tichnor Brothers.*

a term referring to girls who had not yet "come out" in society. The squires were the boys. "Sub-Deb Clubs are particularly popular in the Middle West," wrote *Life* magazine in 1945. "In Indianapolis they are epidemic." Over six thousand young people were members of seven hundred different clubs, which staged skits, held dinners, and sponsored other youth-oriented activities. Ann Zarick was the adviser for the Syrian sub-debs and squires, which was formally associated with the Midwest Federation of Syrian and Lebanese Clubs. Her son was vice president.

Though Zarick's leadership in a regional federation set her apart from many others—male or female—she was only one of many local woman leaders. Helen Freije was president of Binette L'Yom (Women of Today). Florence Freije was president of the Lamba Kappa Psi sorority. Sarah Mikesell was a leader of the Ladies Goodwill Society, associated with the Syrian American Brotherhood.

The establishment of social clubs made it possible for Arab American women in the first half of the 1900s to build local networks, participate in Indianapolis's charitable sector, discuss their duties as citizens, carve out time for leisure, and celebrate both Arab and American dancing, music, and food. Developing clubs that were geared specifically to Syrian and Lebanese people, which constituted most of the Arab American community at the time, was not a way to separate themselves from the rest of Indianapolis society. It was a way to become equal participants in it.

Healing Hoosiers for a Century

In 1938, when Dr. Waheeb Salim Zarick died of a heart attack at the age of forty-three, the city of Indianapolis lost a prominent medical educator and one of its great Arab American leaders.

W. S. Zarick was born in 1894 or 1895 in the city of Tripoli, today located in the modern nation-state of Lebanon, which was then part of the Ottoman Empire. Around the age of seven, Dr. Zarick left this beautiful town overlooking the Mediterranean Sea for Frankfort, Indiana, where he attended public school. He went to college at the University of Michigan and received his MD in 1927 from the Indiana University School of Medicine, where he was a member of Tau Kappa Alpha and the debating team, president of the Cosmopolitan Club, president of the French Circle, and secretary of the Skeleton Club, the student medical club.

Like so many other Arab Americans in the 1920s and 1930s, Dr. Zarick was deeply involved in civic life. He was a member of St. George Syrian Orthodox Church, a leader of the Syrian American Brotherhood, and most significantly, he was the first president of the Midwest Federation of Syrian Clubs.

He must have been a busy man because he also volunteered as president of the Indiana Society of Magicians.

His day job was at the Indiana University School of Dentistry, where he served as an assistant professor of anatomy. In addition, he was a public school physician.

Dr. Zarick was one of the first Arab Americans trained in the United States to become prominent in Indianapolis health care. But he is just one of many who have been healing Hoosiers for a century.

Perhaps it is not an accident that so many Arab and Arab Americans are health care professionals. The field has deep roots in Arab cultures. "The earliest documented general hospital," according

W. S. Zarick taught Anatomy II at the Indiana University School of Dentistry, which first occupied the building pictured here in 1933. *Credit: Edward Curtis.*

to David W. Tschanz, "was built in 805 in Baghdad, [Iraq]." During the Middle Ages, Arab and Persian discoveries in disease treatment, anatomy, pharmacology, and nutrition revolutionized the practice of medicine throughout Africa, Asia, and Europe, where Arabic language medical texts were used to train doctors for hundreds of years.

Arab American physicians have had a significant impact on the way medicine is practiced in the United States too. First, there are the sheer numbers. Tens of thousands of Arab Americans, both Christians and Muslims born abroad and in the United States, are physicians. Though Arab Americans account for a small percentage of Americans overall—perhaps just 1 or 2 percent—it seems safe to conclude, based on studies of Muslim American physicians, that the number of Arab physicians per capita is greater than the number of non-Arab physicians.

Then, there is the quality of their work. One of the most important health leaders in the nation is Dr. Elias Zerhouni, former director of the National Institutes of Health. Other physicians have made pathbreaking contributions to their respective fields. Dr. Nawal Nour changed the way gynecological patients who seek healing for female genital cutting (FGC) are treated. Dr. Michael DeBakey was perhaps "the greatest surgeon ever," according to the *Journal of the American Medical Association* (2005). Dr. Huda Zoghbi explained the genetic mutations associated with Rett Syndrome, a disease that deprives one in 10,000 girls of their "ability to speak, walk, eat, and even breathe easily."

The legacy of Arab American physicians in greater Indianapolis is similarly impressive, as the story of Dr. William K. Nasser illustrates.

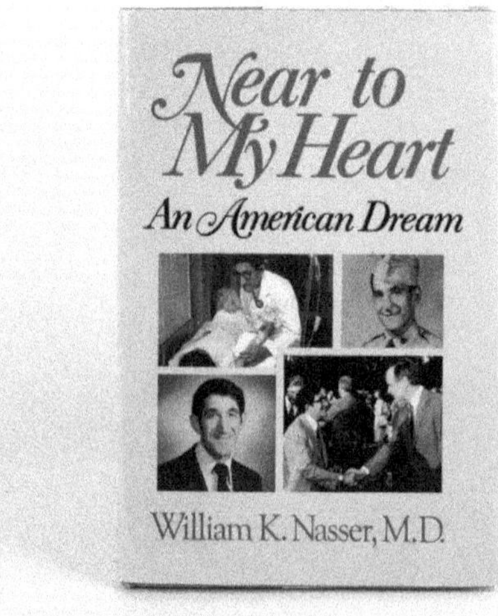

Near to My Heart is the autobiography of Indiana's father of cardiology, the son of Syrian immigrants. *Credit: Ziad Hefni.*

Born in Terre Haute, Indiana, in 1933, Dr. Bill Nasser is sometimes called Indiana's "father of cardiology." His parents, Tawfiq and Mahmoudy Nasser, were Christian immigrants from Damascus, Syria, who made their living as owners of a grocery store. Dr. Nasser, the author of *Near to My Heart: An American Dream*, was a self-described "late bloomer." After serving in the US Army in Korea, he finished his undergraduate degree at Indiana State University. He then completed an MD at the IU School of Medicine, where he also finished a fellowship and taught cardiovascular medicine until the early 1970s.

In 1972, St. Vincent's Hospital asked him to help establish their heart program, which has become one of the largest and most successful cardiology practices in the country. During his lifetime, he received numerous awards for his achievements. Many years after his death, St. Vincent's honored him by opening the William K. Nasser MD Education and Simulation Center, which served as a vaccination site during the COVID-19 pandemic.

Today, it is impossible to imagine health care in Indianapolis without the expertise and labor of Arab American doctors. Look at any hospital in central Indiana and you will find Arab Americans working there.

For example, Dr. Shadia Jalal is an associate professor of clinical medicine and the leading esophageal cancer expert at the Indiana University Melvin and Bren Simon Cancer Center. Among the many clinical trials for new cancer treatments that she has conducted is one that led to the approval of a medicine called pembrolizumab, which works with a patient's immune system to fight esophageal and other cancers. She also conducts research in a laboratory to understand how genetics has an impact on the effectiveness of various cancer treatments. She publishes what she discovers in peer-reviewed journals.

Of all the tasks that she performs, Dr. Jalal is perhaps most grateful that "my patients trust me with their health at their darkest and lowest moments." Dr. Jalal works two days a week at Richard L. Roudebush VA Medical Center, treating military veterans who have various forms of lung cancer. She is "very passionate" about her efforts over the last several years to "build the oncology research program to ensure veterans have access to good clinical trials." Dr. Jalal is also cochair of "the committee that is defining the best medical practices for the treatment of lung cancer at VA hospitals across the country."

Shadia Jalal was born in Minneapolis, Minnesota, to an educated family—her dad was a PhD, her mom was a lawyer. Before she was a year old, her family moved back to Amman, Jordan. She grew up there and finished her MD at the University of Jordan in 2002. She returned to the United States in 2003 to complete her residency in internal medicine at Indiana University and stayed for a fellowship in hematology and oncology.

Dr. Jalal did not enter her residency thinking that she wanted to be a cancer doctor, but then she worked with Dr. Larry Einhorn. "I was amazed by the humility of a man that seems to know everything," she remembers. "I strive to be that kind of teacher and mentor."

She did not expect to settle down in Indiana either, but then she married a Hoosier. "My husband Tarick has Arab roots," she said, "but grew up in Valparaiso, Indiana. He is a podiatrist. We met at Methodist Hospital in 2005 when we needed a podiatry consult for a patient with an infected diabetic foot ulcer." She jokingly chastises herself for not knowing what she was getting into. "I should have known that marrying a Hoosier meant watching way too much football and college basketball!"

In truth, she is very grateful for him, their children, and a career that gives her a chance to try to heal and be present for cancer patients and their family members.

Shadia Jalal is unique, but she is also one of many Arab Americans in central Indiana whose careers focus not so much on themselves, as she puts it, as on their patients.

There is also Mohammad Al-Haddad, who serves as head of gastroenterology and hepatology at the IU School of Medicine; Amale Lteif, who studies thyroid disease; Zeina Nabhan, who treats pediatric diabetes at Riley Children's Hospital; Ahmad Saltagi, who sees people with pulmonary disease and sleep disorders; Mohamad Saltagi, who is an otolaryngology resident at IU School of Medicine; and Taiseer Shatara, who treats patients with gastroenterology disorders. There are so many more. The list of healers goes on and on. Their work represents one of the most profound contributions of Arab Americans to Indianapolis. It is work that makes a community proud of itself.

Dr. Shadia Jalal is a researcher who also treats cancer patients at the IU Simon Cancer Center and Roudebush VA Medical Center. *Credit: Ziad Hefni.*

The Indianapolis Connection to St. Jude's Hospital

In 1957, Arab American actor and comedian Danny Thomas asked a man from Indianapolis to lead the effort to establish a national children's hospital that would treat kids with cancer and other diseases for free. By the time he had finished, Michael Tamer raised $43 million for St. Jude Children's Research Hospital. He had become one of the greatest fundraisers in the United States.

Tamer was born in Appalachia, Virginia, in 1904, but he moved to Indianapolis as a young man in the 1920s. In 1926, his marriage at St. Francis de Sales Church to another Syrian American, Marie Kurker, was featured in the *Indianapolis News* society pages. He became active in the Arab American social scene as he made his living as a salesman. Over his career, he would also own a lamp store, the Red Key Tavern and other bars, and a candy shop. Such work paid the bills, but Mike Tamer's passion was for philanthropy, not business.

In the 1930s, he became leader of the Syrian So-Fra Club, which brought Arab Americans together not only for socializing but also to raise money for charitable causes. Tamer quickly developed a reputation as someone who was good at getting things done. In 1939, he served as chair of the twentieth anniversary of Indianapolis's Syrian American Brotherhood.

During World War II, Tamer led Arab Indianapolis's effort to buy war bonds and support Indianapolis's Arab American men and women in uniform. The various Syrian clubs that had been holding dances and raising money for charity came together at this time to form the Associated Syrian Lebanon Club of Indianapolis. Tamer, whose brother Mitchell died in the war, served as president.

In 1944, Tamer was also elected president of the Syrian American Brotherhood. During the war years, its clubhouse on Riverside Park became a venue for war bonds sales. Visitors were offered free buffets, dancing, and singing, and then they were expected to generously support the war effort. At one event alone, Tamer sold $210,000 in bonds. Members of the military, especially from Fort Benjamin Harrison and Camp Atterbury, were also feted during New Year's and other celebrations at the clubhouse.

Mike Tamer gained a national reputation as a nonprofit leader and a fundraiser, and in 1955, he was elected president of the National Association of Federations of Syrian Lebanese Clubs during a meeting in French Lick. One of his first official duties was leading 325 members of the association as they left for a month-long convention in Syria and Lebanon. During his time in Syria, Prime Minister Sabri al-Assaly and Foreign Affairs Minister Khaled al-Azm awarded him with Syria's medal of merit. Later, Lebanon presented him with its Legion of Honor award at the presidential palace in Beirut.

Mike Tamer, seated, wears his Danny Thomas Open sports jacket in 1969. Tamer and Thomas were close friends. *Credit: Geni.*

Two years later, Danny Thomas tapped Tamer to become the national executive director of the American Lebanese Syrian Associated Charities (ALSAC), the philanthropic organization that funded St. Jude Children's Hospital, which broke ground in 1958. Tamer set up a modest office at 611 Massachusetts Avenue. At first, he worked for free. Aided by LaVonne Rashid, Tamer hit the road, helping ten regional directors establish 142 chapters in thirty-five states. It was the largest Arab American philanthropic organization of its time. Tamer and Rashid became paid employees of ALSAC, and its modest office remained in Indianapolis until 1975, the year after Tamer's death.

Even then, his name lived on at St. Jude Hospital in Memphis, where there is a building named after him and Rashid. There is also the Michael F. Tamer Chair of Biomedical Research on the St. Jude Hospital faculty. These are fitting tributes to the person about whom Danny Thomas once said, "I must thank God that along came Mike Tamer, because without his leadership, St. Jude Children's Research Hospital would have been just a dream."

Ahmed Alamine performs tawaf, or circling, around the Ka'ba in Mecca, the site of the annual hajj, or pilgrimage. Pilgrims like Imam Alamine wear what is called ihram clothing, two simple white sheets wrapped around the waist and the shoulders. *Credit: Ahmed Alamine, 2019.*

PROFILE: Imam Ahmed Alamine

Ahmed Alamine is director of religious affairs at the Indianapolis Muslim Community Association (IMCA), and imam, or leader, of its mosque, Masjid Al-Fajr, the Mosque of the Morning Prayer, the oldest continuously operating Sunni Muslim mosque in the city, dating from the 1970s. In 2020, he was sworn in as the first Muslim police chaplain in the history of the Indianapolis Metropolitan Police Department. He also serves as chaplain with the Marion County Sheriff's Office. Born in Saudi Arabia, Imam Alamine grew up in Medina, the city where, in 622 CE, the Prophet Muhammad sought refuge from Mecca and established the first Islamic government. In this interview, Alamine discusses his upbringing, what led him to Indianapolis, and his experiences as an Arab American of African descent.

Q. Where did you grow up? What was it like? What was your experience there?
A. I was born in Saudi Arabia and lived there until I was about ten years old when my father decided to work for the government of Saudi Arabia in Niger. My experience of living in Saudi Arabia was an amazing experience. We lived next to the Mosque of the Prophet Muhammad, peace be upon him, with our extended families who migrated from Africa. We had great relationships with our neighbors. Although I have experienced some level of racism, the people of Medina are known to be kind, generous, and welcoming. When we moved to Niger, the experience was totally different! It was a mix of cultural shock, a language barrier, and low socioeconomic conditions compared to Saudi Arabia. But Niger and its people are very peaceful and welcoming. This made my adaptation to the Nigerien society seamless.

Q. When did you come to Indianapolis?
A. I came to Indianapolis in 2010 from Columbus, Ohio, at the recommendation of a close friend.

Q. What is your education?
A. I have a BA in Islamic studies, a master's in Islamic economics and banking, and an MBA. I am currently pursuing a third master's in philanthropic studies at Indiana University Lilly Family School of Philanthropy, and I hope to pursue a PhD in international philanthropy and sustainable development.

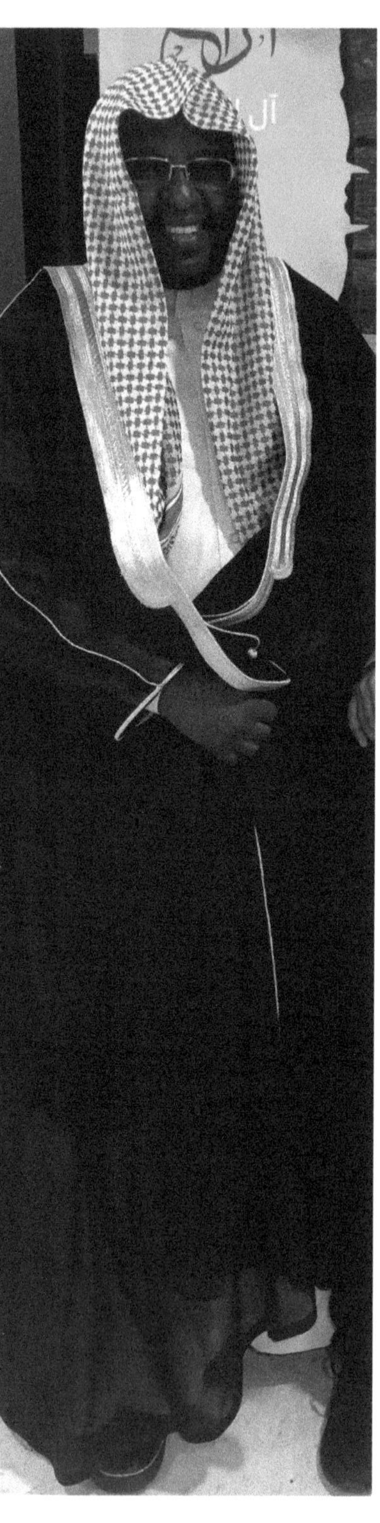

Q. What jobs have you had in Indiana? What are your duties? Why did you choose this as your career?
A. In the business world, I have worked in logistics, quality control, and managerial positions. In the nonprofit sector, I started out by volunteering to teach and give lectures and Friday sermons in Indianapolis-area mosques. Two years before I become the Imam of Masjid Al-Fajr, I volunteered as chair of the religious affairs committee at IMCA. Then, I was asked by the board to be the imam. I have held that position since 2017.

Q. What does your Arab heritage mean to you?
A. It really means a lot to me. In addition to my many other things, my Arab heritage has shaped my identity and personality.

Q. What are the challenges and joys of being an Arab American in Indianapolis?
A. I really cannot recall any major challenges as I have no issues getting along with people from different backgrounds; however, many times I find that I do not fully belong to either African culture as a Black man nor to Arabic culture, which is my primary cultural identity. This has made full assimilation a challenge to a certain degree. However, the big joy is that I have always felt welcome by people of Indianapolis who come from different cultural and ethnic backgrounds. It has been very easy for me to navigate through professional, personal, and social life.

Q. Many Americans—and for that matter, many Arabs—do not think that you can be both Black and Arab. How do you think of your own identity when it comes to race?
A. When people ask me where I am from, I almost always tell them, sarcastically, that I have an identity

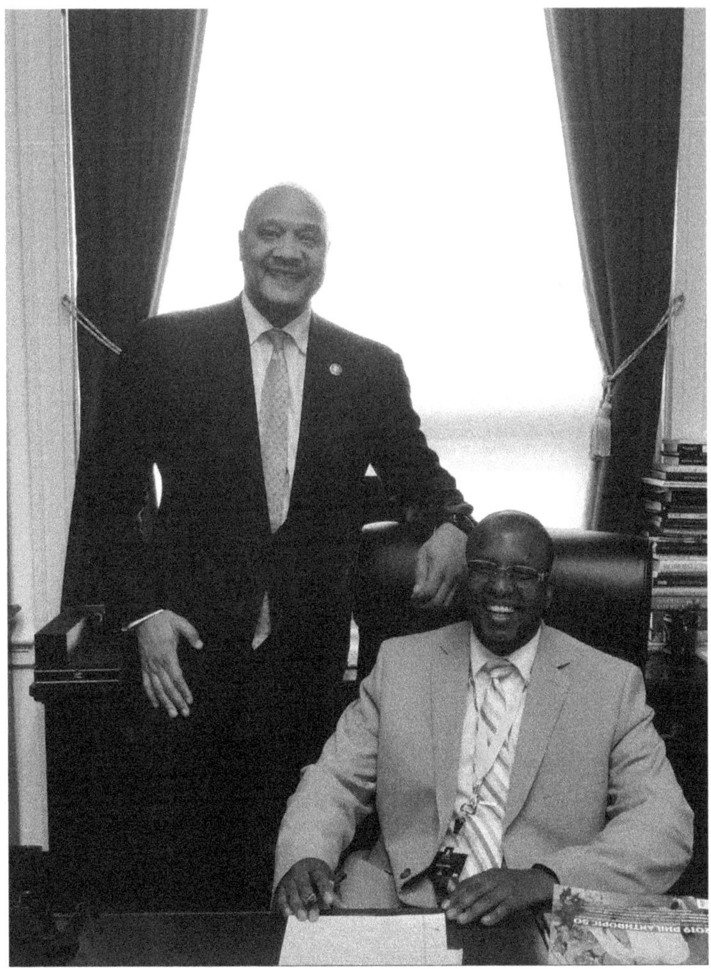

Above: In 2019, Imam Alamine visited US Representative André Carson, the second Muslim elected to US Congress. Carson represents most of the city of Indianapolis. *Credit: Ahmed Alamine.*

Previous page: Like other Saudi men, Imam Ahmed Alamine sometimes wears a red and white hatta, or headscarf, and a bisht, a gold-lined cloak. *Credit: Ahmed Alamine.*

crisis. My parents are Africans who migrated to Saudi Arabia at a very early age with my grandparents. When I tell people that I was born in Saudi Arabia, the response often is, "I did not know that they have Black people there!" So being Black with Arabic and African heritage makes it challenging to fit in anywhere. At the same time, the diversity of my cultural background—which allows me to speak five different languages fluently—is my greatest asset.

salesforce
INDIANA WORLD WAR MEMORIAL

CHAPTER THREE

ARAB INDIANAPOLIS IN WORLD AFFAIRS

Though Indianapolis has been stereotyped as an isolated and monolithic city in America's heartland, the state's capital has always been connected to and affected by events beyond the borders of the United States. America's foreign wars have been particularly important to the city's history, and Indianapolis is known nationally for memorializing those Hoosiers who sacrificed their lives in those conflicts. Arab Americans are among those whose names are recorded in the city's war memorials. But beyond serving in the US military, Arab Americans in Indianapolis have been affected by the vicissitudes of world affairs in ways unfamiliar to many of their Indiana neighbors. Colonialism, military occupation, and political upheaval across North Africa and the Middle East have resulted in both voluntary immigration and the forced settlement of Arabic-speaking people to Indianapolis for more than a century.

Arab Americans in the Two World Wars

World War I cut off immigration from the Arabic-speaking world. Many Arab Americans who had thought that they might one day return to the Arab world decided to become US citizens. One way of earning that citizenship was through military service. According to the US War Department, 13,965 Syrian Americans—something like 7 to 14 percent of the total Syrian American population—wore the uniform during World War I. But there were other reasons why serving in the military was viewed in a positive light. Christian and Muslim Syrians, citizens of the Ottoman Empire, generally favored the movement for Syrian independence

The Indianapolis World War I Memorial includes a shrine to fallen service members. *Credit: Ziad Hefni.*

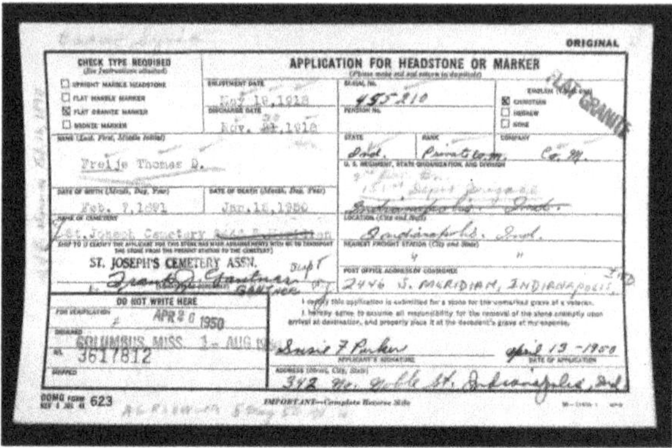

ORIGINAL

APPLICATION FOR HEADSTONE OR MARKER

CHECK TYPE REQUIRED
FLAT GRANITE MARKER

ENLISTMENT DATE: May 19, 1918
SERIAL NO. 455 210
DISCHARGE DATE: Nov. 30, 1918
CHRISTIAN
FLAT GRANITE
NAME (Last, First, Middle Initial): Freije Thomas D.
STATE: Ind.
RANK: Private
COMPANY: Co. M.
DATE OF BIRTH: Feb. 7, 1891
DATE OF DEATH: Jan. 16, 1950
151st Depot Brigade
NAME OF CEMETERY: St. Joseph Cemetery
LOCATION: Indianapolis, Ind.
ST. JOSEPH'S CEMETERY ASSN.
POST OFFICE ADDRESS OF CONSIGNEE: 2446 S. MERIDIAN, INDIANAPOLIS
DO NOT WRITE HERE
APR 20 1950
COLUMBUS MISS. 1 AUG
3617812
Susie F Parker
APPLICANT'S SIGNATURE
April 13 - 1950
DATE OF APPLICATION
342 No. Noble St. Indianapolis, Ind.
QMG FORM 623
IMPORTANT—Complete Reverse Side

Thomas Freije, like others who served in the military, was eligible for a military headstone. He was buried at St. Joseph's Cemetery in Indianapolis. *Credit: National Archives.*

from the Ottomans. Because the Ottomans were allies to the Germans in World War I, many Syrian Americans hoped that the defeat of the Ottomans at the hands of the British, French, and Americans would result in freedom for Syria.

Some Arab Americans served in the US military because it was law. Among their number was Indianapolis resident Thomas D. Freije, who was born around 1891 in the village of Zahlé, located in the Bekaa Valley of what today is Lebanon. When he registered for the draft in 1917, Thomas Freije was already a naturalized citizen of the United States, which meant that he had to serve if called. He claimed an exemption because he needed to take care of his parents. His father, David Frieje, was around seventy years old, and Thomas managed the family grocery store. Thomas Frieje also said he had broken a leg in three places. Uncle Sam told him to report for duty anyway. He served from May 19 to November 30, 1918, in the 151st Depot Brigade, preparing troops to deploy for battle in France.

Today, if you walk the long stairs up and down the World War I Memorial in downtown Indianapolis, you can see his name listed among those of the many Hoosiers who served in what was called the Great War.

Perhaps 15,000 or more Arab Americans served in the US military during World War II, and Arab Indianapolis was anxious to do its part. On the home front, there were dances and other fundraisers to support the troops, patriotic speeches to demonstrate the loyalty of Arab Americans to the country, and meetings at the Syrian American Brotherhood and other places to sell war bonds to pay for the war. Many in Arab Indianapolis put their bodies on the line in combat too, and some of them made the ultimate sacrifice.

US Army Technician Fourth Grade James Camill Haboush was just twenty-two years old when he died on the field of battle. Born in Indianapolis on November 24, 1922, he was the child of Syrian immigrants. His father immigrated before World War I from Aitanite, a tiny village in the Bekaa Valley located near the Litani River. His mother did not come to the United States until 1920. She was from Mashghara, a nearby town. When he was a boy, Camill's father, also named James, worked as a machinist at a railroad car shop, while his mother, Edna, was a homemaker. In the 1930s, the family joined the ranks of Indianapolis's Syrian grocers as proprietors of H & B Market on 2706 Southeastern. They lived nearby at 2510 Southeastern, next door to a Methodist church and just a couple blocks south of the PCC and St. Louis Railroad yard.

Camill attended Arsenal Tech High School and also worked in his parents' grocery store. In 1938, the year before Hitler invaded Poland, he composed a poem that eerily foreshadowed a time when he would give up play-fighting for the real thing. He was about sixteen when he penned "Days of the Saber," which was featured in the high school yearbook, *The Arsenal Cannon*.

> Oh, those were the days of my childhood joys,
> Me and my gang of barefoot boys.
> We sailed the seas in a rocking chair.
> The tales we told would stiffen the hair.
> We needed a ship to fight with Drake.
> So, for a mast we used a rake.
> On a chair for a cabin stood
> My sister's dollhouse made of wood.
> Our blood sabers we'd swing through the air.
> If mother hid the catsup, our sabers were bare.
> Oh, those were the days of my childhood joys!
> We had good times, me and my barefoot boys.

Camill Haboush came from a patriotic family. As President Roosevelt put the US on a war footing after 1939, many immigrants became anxious to show that they would be loyal to the United States. In 1941, the local chapter of the Defenders of Democracy staged a rally and parade, inviting Serbians, Greeks, Romanians, and Syrians—Hoosiers whose presence still provoked anxiety among the white, Protestant majority—to join in. As a member of the board of directors of the Syrian American Brotherhood, which was a strong supporter of the war, James Haboush, Camill's father, was selected to serve on the planning committee.

Indianapolis residents who perished in World War II are memorialized, like those who died in World War I, at the Indiana War Memorial Plaza Historic District, which has more monuments to fallen service members than any other place outside the nation's capital. *Credit: Ziad Hefni.*

OF THOSE WHO SERVED

Camill Haboush was one of a dozen people with his same last name to register for service. One of them was his brother Victor. Camill served in the infantry of the Sixth Army, which was responsible in 1943 and 1944 for expelling Japanese military forces from New Guinea and securing the island as a base for further military operations in the Pacific. In October 1944, the Sixth Army began its invasion of the Japanese-occupied Philippines. That month, James Camill Haboush died "in the line of fire," as his US Army hospital admittance papers said.

Half a world away, Mitchell Tamer would make the same sacrifice for his country.

Mitchell Tamer was born July 11, 1916, in Appalachia, Virginia. He was the son of Frank and Mary Tamer, who came to the United States in 1892 from Zahlé, located today in Lebanon's Bekaa Valley. They were Melkite Christians, sometimes called Greek Catholics, who used an Orthodox-like liturgy in their worship service but aligned themselves with the Roman Catholic Church. Frank made his living as a dry goods salesman. His mother passed away in 1925, and his father moved to Kentucky, but a couple of his brothers settled down in Indianapolis. Mitchell lived with his brother, Michael, who was one of Arab Indianapolis's most active community volunteers in the 1930s. Mitchell was socially active too, participating in the Syrian So-Fra Club and attending meetings at the Syrian American Brotherhood.

Three of the Tamer brothers served during the war. Lieutenant A. F. Tamer was stationed in Hawai'i. Private First Class Samuel F. Tamer was reportedly located in the European theater of operations. Michael Tamer, who would later become well-known as a key figure in the founding of St. Jude Children's Research Hospital in Memphis, stayed home to become one of Arab Indianapolis's most successful fundraisers for the war effort.

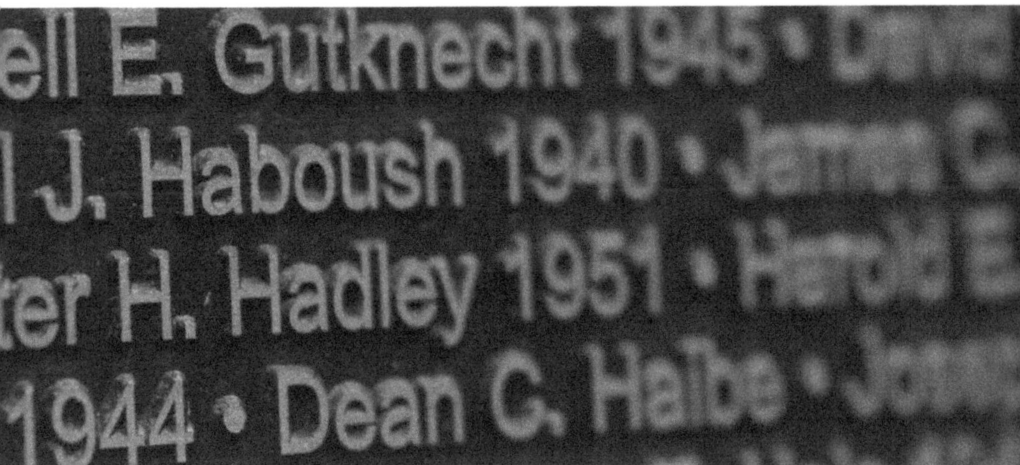

Arsenal Tech High School in Indianapolis has memorialized its students who died in military service. Camill Haboush is one of several Arab Americans who attended school there. *Credit: Vinnie Manganello.*

Zahléh, village d

Mitchell Tamer enlisted on August 11, 1941, at Fort Benjamin Harrison. His regiment left in 1942 for Tidworth Barracks in England. More than a year and a half later, on June 6, 1944, the battle to liberate the European continent from Nazi Germany began on the beaches of Normandy. This was D-Day. On June 7, Private Mitchell Tamer's regiment joined the fight. He was part of the 175th Infantry Regiment, 29th Infantry Division. Some of them landed on Omaha Beach. They marched from the seaside, sometimes facing intense resistance from German forces. They captured Lison on June 9. On July 24, Private Tamer was promoted to corporal. He performed the jobs of both mortar crewman and field artillery crewman, perhaps supervising others when he became corporal. The regiment fought throughout Normandy and then was assigned to help in the Battle of Brest. On August 30, 1944, Mitchell Tamer, twenty-eight years old, was killed in action.

He was buried in the Brittany American cemetery in Normandy, France, with thousands of other service members who lost their lives in the Normandy and Brittany campaigns. He was also remembered at home. On September 26, 1944, family and friends attended a requiem mass for Mitchell Tamer at Little Flower Roman Catholic Church.

Mitchell Tamer and Camill Haboush were two of over twelve thousand service members from Indianapolis who gave their lives in World War II.

Frank and Mary Tamer's children were born in the United States, but Frank and Mary immigrated from the town of Zahlé, pictured here in the 1800s. *Credit: Maison Bonfils, Wiki Commons.*

Palestinian Hoosiers

Today, about half of all Palestinians live outside their traditional homeland, which is located in Israel, the Israeli-occupied West Bank, and the Gaza Strip. Perhaps 250,000 of them have settled in the United States. Though relatively small in number, they have made extraordinary contributions to Greater Indianapolis, especially in medicine, education, public service, and entrepreneurship. Among their number is Fady Qaddoura, the first Arab American Muslim elected to the Indiana Senate.

Palestinians have made their homes in Indianapolis for more than a century. John Haramy, for example, was born around 1894 in Jerusalem, which was then ruled by the Ottoman Empire, and arrived in the United States in 1913. He attended Earlham College in Richmond, Indiana, served in the US Army during World War I, became a naturalized US citizen, and briefly returned to Palestine to teach school before settling in Indianapolis in the early 1920s.

For about two decades, he was a professor at Indiana Central College, today known as the University of Indianapolis. He began his career at the college as a French professor and debate coach but eventually became head of the history and social science department.

In addition to completing his law degree at Indianapolis's Benjamin Harrison Law School, which would merge with IU Law School in 1936, Haramy worked on his master's and doctorate in history while serving as a professor. His 1937 Indiana University PhD dissertation was entitled *The Palestine Mandate: A Study in Conflicting Interests.*

Like many professors working at teaching colleges, John Haramy did not publish his research in journals or books. Instead, he shared his ideas and knowledge in the classroom and in countless public lectures across the state of Indiana. He was a "gifted

In 1937, John Haramy was one of thirty-five instructors included in the Indiana Central College yearbook. *Credit: University of Indianapolis* Oracle.

HN A. CUMMINS
Philosophy
Otterbein College 1887
Otterbein College 1890
. Indiana Central 1911

LYLE J. MICHAEL
Chemistry
B.S. Otterbein College 1919
M.S. Ohio State University 1920
Ph.D. Ohio State University 1929

LEORA WEIMAR
Speech and Journalism
A.B. Indiana Central 1921
A.M. Northwestern University School of Speech 1929

VIRGINIA CRAVENS
English and Dean of Women
A.B. Depauw University 1910

SIBYL WEAVER
English
. Indiana Central 1916
I. Indiana University 1918

JOHN J. HARAMY
History and Political Science
A.B. Earlham College 1918
LL.B. Benjamin Harrison Law School 1924
A.M. Indiana University 1926

DAVID H. GILLIATT
Religion
A.B. Indiana Central 1920
B.D. Bonebrake Theological Seminary 1923
A.M. Chicago University 1930
Ph.D. Southern Baptist Theological Seminary 1934

WILLIAM P. MORGAN
Biology
B. Indiana Central 1919
M. Indiana University 1922
.D. Indiana University 1926

HARRY C. GOOD
Physical Education and Athletics
A.B. Indiana Central 1925
M.S. Indiana University 1932

The Abu-Salih family are proud Palestinians and Muslims; on formal occasions, Thara Alzoubi, Dr Abu-Salih's spouse, and their daughters wear the Palestine thawb, which features traditional needlework patterns. *Credit: Majdi Abu-Salih.*

orator" who spoke at high schools, churches, and men's groups, among other places. His topics included dictatorship and democracy, international relations, and American patriotism. In 1936, he was chosen to give the principal address at the official opening of the Syrian American Brotherhood clubhouse.

The speaking bug ran in the family. When his sister, Katrina Haramy, came to Indianapolis in 1939 to visit her brother, she gave dozens of public speeches, addressing church services, Christian women's groups, sororities, and the Daughters of the American Revolution. She spoke of her harrowing travels through Europe as World War II began and of her experience as a teacher at the Ramallah Friends School.

In 1947 and 1948, after leaving his teaching post to become a lawyer and a part-time Quaker minister, her brother John became one of Indiana's most articulate advocates for what today is called the "one-state" solution to the Palestinian-Israeli conflict. He toured the state, speaking against the partition of Palestine into separate Jewish and Arab territories. Arguing that there was no inherent conflict among Palestinian Jews, Christians, and Muslims, he said that all could live in harmony. He blamed European settlers called Zionists for the conflict, and he argued that their political,

Mina and Eloisa Khoury were married in 1977 in St. George Orthodox Church. *Credit: Mina Khoury, St. George Church.*

religious, and economic rationales for a separate Jewish state in Palestine were ill-founded. In 1948, he proposed that the best solution was local rule under the authority of the United Nations.

John Haramy may have been one of the first prominent Palestinian professionals in Indianapolis, but he was not the last. One of the consequences of the 1948 Arab-Israeli war was that Israel, Jordan, and Egypt ended up dividing the land of Palestine among themselves. Palestinians became stateless. Many were forced to move elsewhere.

As refugees or displaced people, their path to Indianapolis could be indirect, as illustrated by the family history of Dr. Majdi Abu-Salih, a pediatric gastroenterologist at Community Health Network. His parents were originally from the Palestinian villages of Ateel and Zeita, near the town of Tulkarm in northern Palestine. From 1948 to 1967, people there lived under the authority of the Hashemite Kingdom of Jordan. There was little opportunity to get ahead, but Dr. Abu-Salih's father was a math whiz. He attended college at the American University of Beirut in Lebanon and then came to the United States for graduate school, studying at the University of Illinois and teaching for a time at Wabash College in Indiana.

Majdi Abu-Salih was born in Urbana, Illinois, shortly after the 1967 Arab-Israeli war in which Israel occupied his parents' villages. One of his uncles was killed, and they were not able to return home. His father took a job in Saudi Arabia, and then the family moved to Jordan, where Majdi Abu-Salih first studied medicine. In 1990, he returned to the country of his birth to finish a residency at the University of Iowa and a fellowship at the University of Michigan before coming to practice medicine, first in Wisconsin and then in Indiana.

Dr. Abu-Salih is not the only Palestinian Hoosier whose life trajectory was affected by the 1967 war. Mina Khoury, the former owner and operator of a Carmel Dairy Queen and other businesses, was compelled to leave his home as a result of the Israeli occupation. "The strict rules and restrictions" of the Israeli military, as well as an economic downturn, led him to seek refuge in Indiana, where his uncle had attended Purdue University in the 1950s. In 1968, he left his hometown, Beit Sahour, the House of the Shepherds. This is the place where Christians believe angels appeared to the shepherds to announce the birth of Jesus in Bethlehem, just a few miles west. Mina and his brother, Alex, became entrepreneurs and found success in the food business in Indiana. Mina also discovered a sense of community at St. George Orthodox Church, where he married his wife, Eloisa, in 1977.

In 1993, the signing of the Oslo Accords between the Israeli government and Palestinian leader Yasser Arafat gave many Palestinians hope that they might finally establish an independent state on the West Bank and the Gaza Strip. Those hopes did not become a reality, however, and by the first decade of the twenty-first century, the peace process failed.

Indianapolis activist Lamese Hasan was there to witness its end. In 2002, the Israeli military laid siege to Palestinian President Yasser Arafat's

Lamese Hasan is an international education consultant who has also volunteered as an activist for Palestinian human rights. *Credit: Ziad Hefni.*

headquarters in Ramallah and used bulldozers to destroy several Palestinian Authority buildings. "I remember the night that Arafat's compound was attacked," she said. "Tanks passed right in front of our house, and I heard bombings and shots fired. There were several times when I feared for my life. I woke to see homes completely destroyed."

Hasan, who works in the field of international student exchange, was born in the United States, but her family had moved back to Palestine when she was thirteen. Her parents, who came from Jerusalem and Al-Bireh, wanted their kids to have the experience of going to an Arab school, living close to their Muslim families, and learning Arabic. Over a period of three years, she also came to understand what life was like under Israeli military occupation. "There were several times when Israeli soldiers would come into our town and issue curfews, arrest innocent Palestinians, and use violence against Palestinians who peacefully protested the occupation," she stated. "We would often visit my mom's side of the family in Jerusalem, and the drive from Ramallah to Jerusalem would become increasingly difficult due to roadblocks, checkpoints, and closures that Israel would randomly implement. I would sometimes be questioned and denied entry into Jerusalem to visit my family or have to take a two-hour roundabout drive to get to my mom's home. It should have taken just fifteen minutes."

When she returned to the United States, she became an activist. Her focus was on human rights. She advocated "freedom of movement, educational opportunities, access to health care, and freedom from daily humiliation and destruction in the form of home demolitions, settlement expansion, and contamination of land and water resources." As a college student, Lamese Hasan organized events and workshops at American University in Washington, DC. She accompanied friends who went to Palestine

Arab Americans and allies rally for Palestinian freedom on May 21, 2021, after Israeli military attacks on Gaza killed 256 people and injured almost two thousand others, according to the United Nations. *Credit: Edward Curtis.*

to witness the impact of the occupation firsthand. She also worked on the ground with activists in Palestine to organize peaceful demonstrations. "I fight for these things not only because I am Palestinian but also because I feel that it is the right of any human to live in dignity, peace, and equality," she declared.

Like Professor John Haramy, Lamese Hasan also became an advocate of the one-state solution. "I personally believe in a one-state solution where all people live under one democracy and are treated equally." The reason, she explained, is that "unfortunately, the two-state solution is no longer viable due to increased [Israeli] settlement expansion that would not allow for a viable Palestinian state."

No matter whether her fellow Hoosiers advocate one state or two states, Lamese Hasan still encourages them to speak up: "It is of the upmost importance for all Americans to join Palestinians in the fight against Israeli occupation not only because it is the right thing to do but because it is US tax dollars that are paying for many of the unjust policies and actions of Israel."

Hope in Exile: An Algerian American Story

In December 1991, Farid Mitiche of Algiers, Algeria, was elected to his country's parliament. On January 12, 1992, one day after it annulled the results of the 1991 elections, the Algerian military sent tanks and troops into the streets of Algiers and began rounding up thousands of political prisoners. "Our party, the Islamic Salvation Front (or FIS), was banned and all its members and followers tracked. Many were killed after being tortured," Mitiche said. Over the next two years, he remembered, "many of my friends and colleagues were sent to concentration camps in the Sahara Desert."

One of the first places where Faouzia Mitiche worked was the MTI School of Knowledge on Cold Spring Road. The largely Muslim student body traces their origins to a wide variety of racial, ethnic, and national backgrounds. *Credit: Ziad Hefni.*

In 2001, Farid and Faouzia Mitiche celebrated the birth of their daughter, Layla. *Credit: Layla Mitiche.*

Farid Mitiche celebrates the *nikah* ceremony of one of his sons. In Islam, the bride and groom sign a nikah, or marriage contract, that spells out a husband's and wife's obligations to one another. *Credit: Layla Mitiche.*

He had to "flee the country to save my life," he said.

Farid Mitiche went underground and then crossed the border illegally into Morocco. It was a terrible blow. "I left my wife behind with our three children, including a newborn of two months." He also left behind the career for which he had worked so hard. Farid Mitiche was not a career politician. He was a surgeon.

His wife, Faouzia Mitiche, also had a degree in medicine. She had grown up in a "very conservative Muslim family" east of Algiers in a "beautiful small town by the beach." It was the kind of place where everyone knew and looked out for one another. "I had a very happy childhood," Faouzia Mitiche said.

In the early 1990s, she said goodbye to the dream of raising her children, as she had been raised, in a happy Algerian home. She waited for word from her husband as he sought political exile in France and Belgium. They would not help him.

Farid Mitiche was surprised but relieved when the United States offered him a visa.

It took two years, but the family reunited in Indianapolis. Two of Faouzia's brothers lived there. Faouzia and Farid Mitiche spoke both French and Arabic, but they had to learn English. It was not easy. "Language was a big barrier for me," Faouzia remembered. "I am still learning English," her husband chuckled.

Faouzia worked as a substitute teacher and taught biology and algebra for a year at MTI School of Knowledge, an Islamic school associated with Al-Fajr Mosque, on Cold Spring Road. She then trained as a cardiac sonographer.

Farid became a cab driver. "Sitting all day at the airport, waiting for fares had . . . a high psychological toll on me," he said. "One day, I was working as a general surgeon, and then suddenly I found myself literally at ground zero, having to start from scratch, learning the ABCs of a new language, accepting any trivial jobs just to get by."

Eventually, he became a medical assistant, then a clinical research coordinator, and more recently, a medical interpreter for French- and Arabic-speaking hospital patients.

It would have been too much without his Islamic faith. "Faith is the essence of my life," he explained. "It is faith that allowed me to navigate through all these years in very troubled waters. It is also faith that helped give sense to the earthquake that shook my life."

Faouzia Mitiche said that even now, she still had not "completely adjusted." She is not alone in that feeling. Exiles and refugees, those violently torn away from their homes, sometimes feel out of place their whole lives. "I still miss my country," she declared. "My siblings, my friends, my culture. I think about it every single day." She would like to return home, but her children are now American, and she would miss them too.

At the same time, Farid and Faouzia Mitiche are deeply thankful to God for one another, for the chance to immigrate to the United States, and especially for their children. Faouzia loves how their children are "so respectful, considerate of others, good Muslims, very intelligent, and kind." Farid admires his kids' commitment to principles over appearances, to sincerity, and to responsibility.

They are also understandably proud of their children's accomplishments. Their daughter, Imen, has a master's in child psychology. Mohammed is getting his doctorate in Islamic studies from the University of Medina. Zakarya is working on his PhD in anthropology from Columbia University. Layla is an IUPUI Honors College student.

Faouzia and Farid hope that their children, their grandchildren, and all those who trace their roots to the Arab world will embrace their heritage and the stories of their ancestors. "I just want them to understand who they are and where they came from," said Faouzia. "The diversity they bring should be perceived not as a handicap but rather as an enrichment to this land," asserted Farid.

Faouzia Mitiche hopes that Arab Americans will be "engaged; active; effective in their community; fight for justice; value education; be proud citizens of the United States." Farid added that while the United States is a land of opportunity, it also suffers from poverty, inequality, racism, and a foreign policy that makes war on too many other countries. Arab Americans should do their part to solve these problems. This is what would "make America great again," Farid joked.

Farid Mitiche's hope for a better, more just, more compassionate country is what got him in trouble in the first place—the good and terrible kind of trouble that led to his and his family's exile from Algeria. But even after the painful experience of displacement, almost two decades later, Farid and Faouzia still believe in that hope—and in the children and the grandchildren that, with God's help, will make it a reality in America, Algeria, and beyond.

PROFILE: Iraqi Poet Sajjad Jawad

Motaz, be patient because Iraq is our Iraq
And we love it in a way that our enemy sees as a strange love
My right hand will forget me if I forget the waters of the Tigris
or a date palm planted on infertile land.

—from "Far or Close" by Sajjad Jawad

Sajjad Jawad, his wife, Methal, and their two boys, arrived in Indianapolis as Iraqi refugees in 2010. The International Organization for Migration (IOM) coordinated their move to the United States. After the 2003 US invasion of Iraq, Mr. Jawad worked with the US National Iraqi Assistance Group, a civil affairs division of the US military, and then with the US Institute of Peace, where he was a senior training program specialist assigned to train Iraqi officials in conflict management skills. Because of his work, he said, "I was granted the special immigrant visa to travel to the United States."

Sajjad Jawad grew up in a family of readers and writers. His uncle is Abdel Khaliq Al Rikabi, an award-winning novelist who wrote *The Filter* and *The Seventh Day of Creation*, among other works. Jawad, who attended the University of Baghdad, drank from the same well of contemporary Arabic literature. He is not a professional writer but an amateur in the best sense. He loves the written word, and much of his life has been devoted to translating people's thoughts, feelings, and experiences into different idioms and languages.

Sajjad Jawad has used those skills to guide others through the many levels of American bureaucracy essential to creating a new life in the United States. As he explained, from the moment he arrived in Indianapolis, "I volunteered to help people at the Families and Social Services Administration office, schools, banks, hospitals, courts, and the Bureau of Motor Vehicles. In one case, I stayed with another

Credit: Ziad Hefni.

Sajjad Jawad and his sons, Ahmed and Mohammed, visit their favorite Iraqi restaurant in Michigan. *Credit: Sajjad Jawad.*

Iraqi in the emergency room from 3:00 p.m. until 7:00 a.m. next day." He also helped others figure out how to use individual development accounts, which are designed to assist people with low incomes save money for a home purchase or education. That's how his own family became homeowners.

Sajjad Jawad praises all those who smoothed his transition to the United States. "Indianapolis warmly welcomed my family and me," he said. A local mosque gave them two cars—he won't name the mosque out of respect for their desire to remain anonymous. One of his son's teachers at Nora Elementary School also donated a used car for the family's use.

His volunteering eventually led to paid employment at Catholic Charities Indianapolis Refugee and Immigrant Services. Sajjad Jawad's first job was to continue the kind of work he did as a volunteer. "In March 2012," he said, "I became the manager of employment services." Then, three years later, he was promoted to supervisor of employment services.

His wife, Methal, is still learning English, but she is such a hard worker that, even without language proficiency, she has become the kitchen manager at a local Chick-Fil-A. She and Sajjad are proud of their two boys, Mohammed and Ahmed, both of whom have been educated in Indianapolis.

His only regret about living in the Circle City is the relative dearth of Iraqi-style Arab food. He particularly misses Iraqi preparations of shawarma, kebab, tikka (which other Arabs sometimes call shish taouk) and quzi, often known as the Iraqi national dish. He sometimes travels to Detroit to eat at his favorite Iraqi restaurant.

He also misses the land of his birth and his extended family members who live in Iraq. His poem "Far or Close" speaks of how they remain close to his heart even as they are physically far away. In 2018, he displayed this poem in both Arabic and English on Indianapolis's Monument Circle as part of the Community Competition to Prevent Islamophobia. The poem is addressed to two of his nephews and to his niece, who is all grown up now—she is a physician and a mother. "Far or Close" is full of longing, but it is also a sweet, intimate embrace of a country often associated with violence and destruction rather than the life-giving properties of its rivers and its people.

Brick Street Poetry curated the "Muslim Voices in Indianapolis" public poetry exhibit on Monument Circle in 2018 in which Sajjad Jawad's "Far or Close" appeared. *Credit: Helen Townsend.*

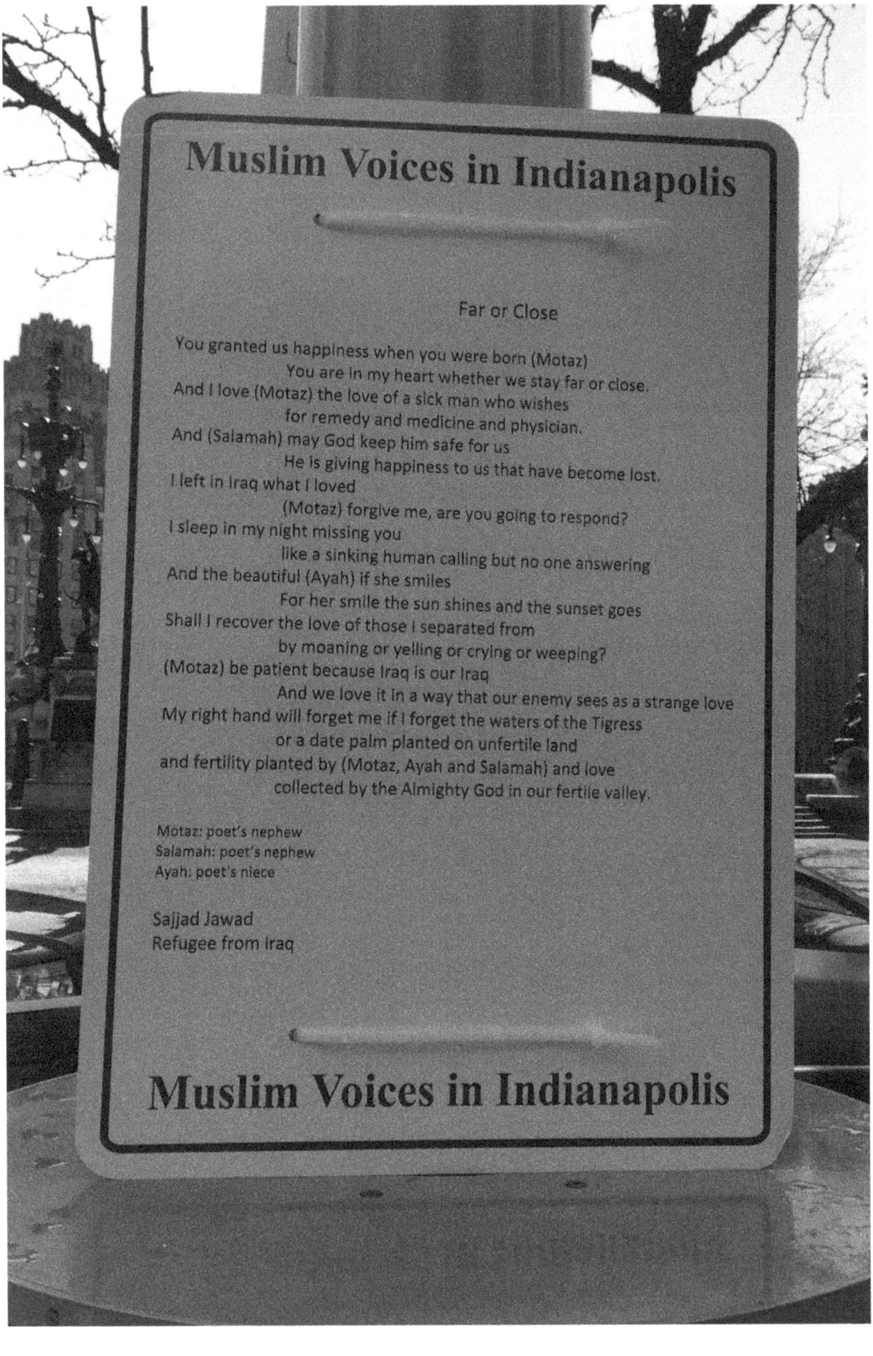

Muslim Voices in Indianapolis

Far or Close

You granted us happiness when you were born (Motaz)
You are in my heart whether we stay far or close.
And I love (Motaz) the love of a sick man who wishes
for remedy and medicine and physician.
And (Salamah) may God keep him safe for us
He is giving happiness to us that have become lost.
I left in Iraq what I loved
(Motaz) forgive me, are you going to respond?
I sleep in my night missing you
like a sinking human calling but no one answering
And the beautiful (Ayah) if she smiles
For her smile the sun shines and the sunset goes
Shall I recover the love of those I separated from
by moaning or yelling or crying or weeping?
(Motaz) be patient because Iraq is our Iraq
And we love it in a way that our enemy sees as a strange love
My right hand will forget me if I forget the waters of the Tigress
or a date palm planted on unfertile land
and fertility planted by (Motaz, Ayah and Salamah) and love
collected by the Almighty God in our fertile valley.

Motaz: poet's nephew
Salamah: poet's nephew
Ayah: poet's niece

Sajjad Jawad
Refugee from Iraq

Muslim Voices in Indianapolis

CHAPTER FOUR
LEADERSHIP

Community leaders such as Ann Zarick and Mike Tamer profoundly shaped the contours of life inside the Arab Indianapolis community. Their contributions, and the success of Arab Hoosiers overall, paved the way for the emergence of men and women who became leaders not just of other Arab Americans but of all Indiana residents as well. Some of them are famous; others are virtually unknown. Their stories reveal how the religiously and politically diverse Arab Indianapolis community has made an impact on the place they call home.

Helen Corey, Reporter

Helen Corey was perhaps the most noteworthy Arab American leader in central Indiana during the 1960s and 1970s. More than four decades before Mitch Daniels became Indiana governor, she was the first Arab American to hold a statewide elected office.

Born in 1923 in Canton, Ohio, her Syrian parents, Maheeba ("Mabel") and Mkhyal ("Mike") Corey, were originally from the Damascus area. She was raised to embrace both Arab and American cultures in addition to the family's Antiochian Orthodox Christian roots. "When my sister, brother, and I were children," she wrote, "our parents sent us to the Orthodox church hall following grade school classes where we learned to read and write the [Arabic] language from Arabic scholars Yusuf (Joseph) Sabb and Hunna (John) Shaheen. Our first lesson taught us that this was one of the richest languages in the world." When the family was around Arabic-speaking friends, they used Arabic names and titles. Brother Albert was Abdullah. Her father was Boo Abdullah, or "the father of Albert," and her mother was addressed by the title Im Abdullah, or "the mother of Albert."

> When we lived in Canton, Ohio, as children, my sister, brother, and I used to get a great deal of pleasure watching my father and his friends take turns smoking the narghileh (Turkish water pipe) as they relaxed during the evenings, exchanging stories of their journey to this country. The narghileh had the sound of bubbling water and an incense aroma filled the house from the Persian tobacco that was used. Our narghileh was made of beautiful cut glass with an oriental brass stem, and the smoking pipe that was attached had an almost cobra look

> with its many variegated colors. . . . The guests were served Turkish coffee and the hostess was ready to play the part of fortuneteller. The cups were inverted and left to stand so that the coffee sediment formed a pattern on the inside of the cup. Then the cups were turned up again and the hostess interpreted the future of each guest from the pattern in his cup.
>
> —Helen Corey, *The Art of Syrian Cookery* (1962)

Around 1947, the family moved to Terre Haute, which was home to a sizeable and active Syrian community. Helen Corey's political career began in 1948 when she worked as the secretary to the city's longest serving mayor, Ralph Tucker. She would hold that position until 1961.

This job provided her with a platform and the connections she needed to become active in the Indiana Democratic Party. In 1956, Corey directed the speaker's bureau of the Indiana Democratic State Central Committee, and in 1959, she was voted Indiana's Outstanding Young Democratic Woman. On October 25, 1960, she was part of Vigo County's welcoming committee for then Senator John F. Kennedy, the Democratic Party's candidate for US President. As a Young Democratic National Committeewoman, she was chosen to greet the "Kennedy Caravan" as it motored its way through Indiana and Illinois. She was also elected Indiana's Young Democrat National Committeewoman and represented the state at the 1960 Democratic National Convention in Los Angeles.

Among the dishes featured on the cover of Helen Corey's 1962 classic are meat pies, stuffed grape leaves, raw kibbi, stuffed zucchini, assorted pastries, and fried kibbi. In the upper right corner, there is a water pipe. *Credit: Ziad Hefni.*

Helen Corey was going places. In 1961, she became director of the Bureau of Women and Children in the Indiana Division of Labor. She offered written guidance to Indiana employers on child labor laws and women's issues in the workplace. She consulted with members of the Indiana General Assembly.

It is almost unbelievable that, as she was working hard for the state and the Democratic Party, she also found the time to pen one of the most influential cookbooks on Syrian food ever written in English. Published by New York's Doubleday in its series on global cuisines, *The Art of Syrian Cookery* (1962) stayed in print for decades. By the middle of 1965, it had sold more than 17,000 copies. Its influence could be felt across North America. Many fans kept it as an essential reference in their kitchen. Food writers from Los Angeles to Miami mentioned it in their columns. Syrians and other Arabs checked it out from their local public libraries. One Arab American in Morgan City, Louisiana, said that "it was as near as mama's cooking as anything I have ever read." Two decades after its publication, in 1982, a well-known Lebanese cook in Montreal, Quebec, explained that though her grandmother taught her to cook, she also relied on *The Art of Syrian Cookery.*

The book was dedicated to Corey's mother, Maheeba, who not only shared the technical aspects of how to make such food but also taught Helen and her sister, Kate, about the cultural, religious, and social meanings and functions of everything from araq (anise-flavored brandy) to zalabee (doughnuts). This was food meant to be shared with others on important occasions in the old country and in the new. Corey explained, for example, what dishes are traditionally offered at wedding receptions and during Arab Orthodox Christian celebrations of Easter and the Feast of the Epiphany.

If it had been published today, this nostalgic food memoir might have launched the career of the charismatic and hardworking Helen Corey as a celebrity chef. But it appeared one year before Julia Child made her debut on public television, and most fancy restaurants hired only male chefs at the time.

Cooking had to remain a side gig.

Fortunately, Corey's political career blossomed at the very same moment that the book was published. In 1963, she was appointed executive secretary of the state's Commission on the Status of Women. The next year, she won the Democratic Party's nomination to run for office, and then, Indiana voters elected Corey to be the twenty-third reporter of the Indiana Supreme and Appellate Courts. She received 1,110,390 votes, enough to unseat the incumbent reporter, Virginia Caylor, who got 920,168 votes. Indiana Governor Roger D. Branigin swore her in as the first Arab American statewide officeholder in 1965.

As reporter, Helen Corey's job was to edit, publish, and distribute all of the judicial rulings of the Supreme and Appellate Courts to law libraries, universities, and law offices. She worked with just two staff members in room 416 at the capitol, where Benjamin Harrison once had his office too. The significance of Corey's election as the first Arab American officeholder in Indiana was not lost on the US Department of State, which featured her in its "Life in America" series distributed abroad.

Helen Corey constantly encouraged women to become politically active. In 1965, for example, she was a featured speaker at the Marion County Democratic women's weekend retreat to French Lick. She addressed the Indiana Federation of Democratic Women in 1967.

That year, she was making $12,500 in her post. The job also came with an official parking spot at the capitol, but when Corey was assigned spot number twenty-one instead of spot number twenty-two, Indiana Clerk Kendal Mathews went berserk. He complained to the governor and the motor vehicles commissioner about it, and he parked in Corey's spot even though the parking attendant told him not to. The *Indianapolis Star* dubbed the incident "Coreyography." Corey said the whole thing was ridiculous.

It wasn't the only time her gender became an issue. She was often asked why she wasn't married, and she gave the answer that one had to give at the time: she believed that women should be married but that they could have a career too. Her good looks were also frequently addressed in public; the *Indianapolis News* referred to her as a "model" and a "pixie politician."

When Helen Corey stood for reelection in 1968, she campaigned hard, giving four speeches a day and traveling over three thousand miles throughout the state to ask for Hoosiers' votes. But with the exception of Democratic US Senator

In 1966, John Daniluck, Frank Kafoure, Helen Corey, Father Joseph Shaheen, and Edith Mesalam were among those who presented Indiana Governor Branigin with a commemorative license plate celebrating the state's sesquicentennial and the fortieth anniversary of the founding of St. George Orthodox Church. *Credit: St. George Church.*

Birch Bayh, Republicans dominated statewide offices that year. Helen Corey's opponent, Marilou Wertzler, got 1,067,357 votes. Corey received 925,616.

After leaving office, Corey remained active with Democratic women's causes, but by the middle 1970s, she turned her attention, at least in part, to political organizing on behalf of Arab American causes. Arab issues were front and center in US public life at the time. For example, in 1973, the Organization of Petroleum Exporting Countries (OPEC) stopped selling oil to nations that supported Israel in its dispute with Egypt. This embargo caused fuel shortages in the United States. Despite the fact that OPEC included non-Arab countries such as Iran and Venezuela—not to mention the fact that most Arab countries are not large oil producers—Arabs in general were blamed for making Americans wait in lines at gas stations. Prejudice and discrimination against Arab Americans increased. The social acceptance that Arab-descended Americans had achieved was now at risk.

Second- and third-generation Arab Americans established the National Association of Arab Americans (NAAA) to lobby national legislators on the foreign issues that affected their lives and livelihoods. One of its programs was "A Day on the Hill," during which Arab Americans from each state would travel to Washington to meet with their members of Congress. Helen Corey was an obvious choice to coordinate the effort in Indiana. Working with George Halaby, Zeldia Hanna, Vicki Mesalam, and Faye Williams, she kicked off the Central Indiana NAAA chapter's effort to gain members with a huge hafli (party) at the Stouffer Hotel in 1975. It featured Arab dancing, music, and food.

Over time, the membership of the NAAA decreased as the American Arab Anti-Discrimination Committee became the largest Arab American national organization. But Helen Corey and other Arab Hoosiers still fought anti-Arab prejudice. In 1990, future Vice President Mike Pence, then a candidate for the US Congress, ran a racist campaign ad in which a white actor donned Arab headgear, a black robe, and dark sunglasses, and used a fake Arab accent to imply that Democrats were unwitting collaborators of the country's Arab enemies. Helen Corey spoke out. "It's degrading a culture," she said, explaining that the use of racial stereotyping would drive many voters away. (Pence defended the ad.)

In the final decades of the 1900s, Helen Corey did not focus as much on explicit political organizing as she did on culinary diplomacy. A leading authority on Syrian and Lebanese food and cooking, Corey used food not only to bridge ethnic differences among Americans but also to educate Americans about her Antiochian Orthodox Christian faith. In 1990, she self-published her second cookbook, *Food from Biblical Lands*, and made a seventy-minute documentary

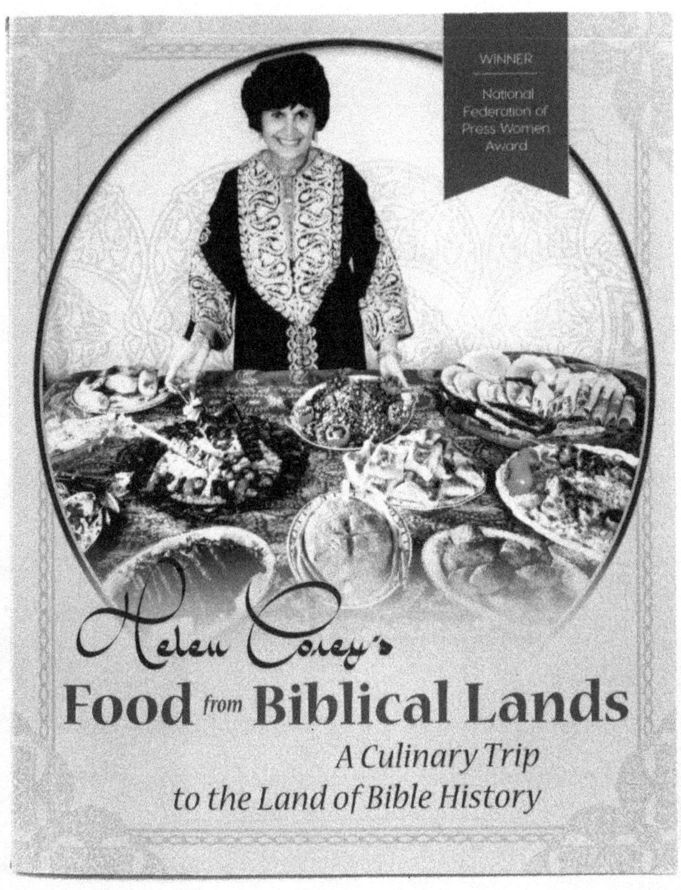

Helen Corey's later cookbooks included meatless menus and an emphasis on the health benefits and Biblical origins of a Mediterranean diet. *Credit: Ziad Hefni.*

to promote it. In 2004, she published *Healthy Syrian and Lebanese Cooking*. These books repeated some of the original recipes from the 1962 classic but also incorporated new dishes from Egypt, Jordan, Morocco, and Palestine. There were also new stories of Corey's travels in Syria and new pictures of her family members, including one of her mother's one hundredth birthday party.

During her long career, Helen Corey gained recognition and respect for her people, for her culture, and for herself. She is one of the most remarkable Hoosiers of Arab descent in history.

Mitch Daniels, Governor

"I'm sure, as a good Syrian, he ran a very honest numbers racket."

—Mitch Daniels, May 4, 2011,
joking about his grandfather

Mitch Daniels's career is quite well-known in his home state. He served as Senator Richard Lugar's chief of staff and the director of President George W. Bush's Office of Management and Budget. He also held an executive position at Eli Lilly and Company and led Purdue University. Most importantly, he was in the governor's mansion for two terms.

But most Hoosiers, it's probably fair to say, are not aware that the forty-ninth governor of Indiana, Mitchell Elias Daniels Jr., is an American of Syrian descent.

Traditionally, Arabic-speaking immigrants and their heirs have been as likely to support Republicans as they have Democrats. Some of the most prominent Arab American politicians have been Republican, including US Senator James Abdnor, US Senator and Secretary of Energy Spencer Abraham, Governor and White House Chief of Staff John Sununu, and US Representative and Secretary of Transportation Ray LaHood.

Like most of these politicians, Mitch Daniels Jr. traces his Arab roots to immigrants who arrived in the United States in the early twentieth century. His grandfather, Elias Daniels, immigrated to the United States from Qalatiyah, Syria, on June 15, 1905.

Qalatiyah is a small, historically Christian village built on rocky but fertile hills about 1,500 feet above sea level. Thirty miles east of the Mediterranean coast, the town has a temperate climate, averaging fifty degrees Fahrenheit in the winter and about eighty degrees in the summer. Its most spectacular attraction, the Krak des Chevaliers, is located five miles south. A crusader castle dating from the

Located north of Lebanon, Krak des Chevaliers is one of Syria's many important historical sites. *Credit: Gianfranco Gazzetti, GAR.*

twelfth century, the impressive ruin is listed as a UNESCO World Heritage Site.

Elias Daniels's destination in America was less bucolic. He settled in Monessen, Pennsylvania, arriving just as this small town close to Pittsburgh became a major site of US steel production. Eventually opening a pool hall on Donner Avenue, across the street from several factories, including Pittsburgh Steel, National Tin Plate, and the Page Woven Wire Fence Company, Daniels chose an advantageous spot. He was not only the merchant who figured out that he could supplement his income by giving factory workers a chance to play the numbers. In Monessen, Elias Daniels was also part of an Arabic-speaking community of Christians large enough to establish and maintain their own Orthodox church.

In 1921, the successful, handsome, and smartly dressed Elias Daniels returned to the old country to find a bride. Mitch Daniels's grandmother, Afife, was around nineteen years of age when she wed the thirty-six-year-old. She then sailed with her husband on the beautiful *Olympic* to make a life in America. They settled down in Monessen, and in 1923, Afife gave birth to Mitchell Daniels Sr. She died just a few years later, and Elias brought up his two boys, Mitchell and Russell, on his own. Mitchell Sr. later attended Allegheny College, served in World War II, and then married Dorothy Wilkes in 1948.

Mitchell Daniels Jr. was born the year after his parents were married. The family moved to Atlanta and Bristol, Tennessee, but in the late 1950s, they came to Indianapolis. The man who would become governor was largely educated in Washington Township schools, including Delaware Trails Elementary, Westlane Middle School, and North Central High School, where he served as student body president. He was already obsessed with politics when he won "Outstanding Citizen" at the annual meeting of Hoosiers Boys State.

Mitch Daniels addresses a crowd as the newly elected student council president of North Central High School in Indianapolis. Credit: *North Central Northerner*, 1966.

Student council adds extra activities

ne responsibilities, the disappointments, the joys, and the rows connected with being president of the North Central Student Council confront Mitch Daniels when the former president, Leon Fink, hands over his gavel.

The Daniels's first home was, as Daniels put it, "in the middle of an all-Jewish neighborhood" around Seventy-Third Street and Spring Mill Road, where the Jewish Community Center and several synagogues are located today. Growing up there had a profound influence on Mitch Daniels. In a 2009 speech, the state's governor said that it was "one of the best things that could ever have happened to me. I made some lifelong friends there; all of my buddies, my whole paper route, everybody on the school bus were Jewish guys and girls." He felt a kinship with the Jewish community. He matriculated at Princeton University, he remembered, "on the heels of the Six Day War," when Israel defeated Syria, Lebanon, Jordan, and Egypt, and occupied the Golan Heights, the West Bank, and the Sinai Peninsula. "Everybody was thrilled with what Israel had accomplished on its own behalf," he recalled. "It was like America had survived or successfully defended itself."

This was a remarkable statement coming from an Arab American. While most in the community mourned the loss of life and land and another setback to the movement for Palestinian self-determination, Mitch Daniels was celebrating. This was not the only time that his views would differ from the majority of Arab Americans. He has been critical of the movement for Palestinian freedom even when it has adopted nonviolent strategies for liberation. Though he was happy to accept the Najeeb Halaby Award for Public Service from the Arab American Institute, Daniels has never been a strong advocate for Arab American issues, and he has not been active in Arab American community affairs. His life and career are useful reminders of the diversity of Arab Indianapolis. There is no one way of being Arab—the Arab American heritage runs in multiple political directions.

Mitch Daniels explained the state and federal aid available to tornado and flood victims in Indiana in 2008. He was accompanied by (left to right) US Small Business Administration Deputy Jovita Carranza, Major General Marty Umbarger, Representative Michael Pence, FEMA Administrator R. David Paulison, Representative Steve Buyer, and FEMA Coordination Officer Mike Smith. *Credit: Barry Bahler/FEMA.*

As he pointed out himself in his speech to the Arab American Institute, his success was predicated on the sacrifices of his Syrian grandparents, the people who made it possible for Mitch Daniels Sr. and Mitch Daniels Jr. to live a life of opportunity.

Fady Qaddoura, State Senator

In 2020, Democrat Fady Qaddoura unseated Republican incumbent State Senator John Ruckelshaus to become the first Arab Muslim legislator in the history of Indiana.

It was an almost unbelievable feat. Ruckelshaus raised $1.9 million for his campaign; Qaddoura had $708,000. Ruckelshaus came from an Indiana Republican family that changed the course of US history; Qaddoura, the son of a homemaker and taxi driver, was raised in the Israeli-occupied West Bank.

Winning this race was the stuff that dreams are made of.

Fady Qaddoura has always been a dreamer, even when many other people might have given up on dreams.

He was born in 1980 to a family from Ramallah, a Palestinian city located north of Jerusalem that was conquered by Israel in the 1967 Arab-Israeli war. The people in Fady Qaddoura's hometown lived under military rule; they were not afforded the basic civil rights that many Americans take for granted. Palestinians eventually revolted against this military occupation in what was called the *intifada*, or shaking off. It started in 1987, when Fady was just a boy. In 1993, Israeli and Palestinian leaders signed a peace agreement called the Oslo Accords, and there was hope that a viable, independent Palestinian state would be established. Palestinian exiles returned to Ramallah, which became known to some locals as the internet café capital of the world.

Fady Qaddoura, who grew up in Ramallah, Palestine, became senator for Indiana district thirty in 2020. *Credit: Ziad Hefni.*

dream into reality. First, however, he needed a job. He became director of health care research and information systems at the University of Texas Medical School, and he ended up finishing his master's in 2007. Then, he volunteered for the Community Development Division of Houston's Muslim American Society chapter. During this time, he managed a budget of $5 million and oversaw eleven staff members. He also completed a certificate at Rice University's Leadership Institute for Nonprofit Executives.

In 2009, he came to Indianapolis to continue his education in public policy and nonprofit management, eventually earning a PhD at IUPUI in 2018. He also won an Islamic Society of North America fellowship to intern at the Indiana General Assembly. That experience launched his career in state and local government. For the last decade, Fady Qaddoura has gone from success to success, from the Indiana Department of Workforce Development and Office of Medicaid Planning to the Division of Health Care Strategies and Technology. In 2016, he became Indianapolis city controller and in 2019, he began campaigning for a seat in the Indiana Senate.

As a candidate, Fady Qaddoura proudly identified as a Muslim. In one campaign photo, his spouse, Samar, and two daughters wear a hijab, or headscarf. On November 17, 2020, he took his oath to the US and Indiana Constitutions with his hand placed on the Qur'an, held by Samar.

"In the Middle East," the newly elected senator told a reporter, "people take care of one another, even with limited resources, with love and compassion for their neighbor." The dreamer from Ramallah wanted to work for that goal in his adopted country, the United States.

"When I die," he told an audience in 2018, "I want people to remember me as the guy who helped them unlock their potential and change the world." It may have sounded a little corny, but it was earnest.

ERRATUM

At the top of page 130, the following text should be added:

Like many mothers and fathers in Palestine, Fady Qaddoura's parents wanted to give their children the best chance possible to succeed in life. They sent their sons Fareed, Fady, and Shadi to the Ramallah Friends School, perhaps the most prestigious high school in the West Bank. Founded in 1869 by Quakers, the school has educated several prominent Palestinian public figures. Its mission is to provide students with an "academically rigorous" education of the highest quality while guiding them to live a "spiritual life" committed to the equality and potential of all people.

In 2000, after graduating, Fady Qaddoura left Palestine to study at the University of New Orleans, where he got his BS in computer science. His brother, Fareed, who obtained his bachelor's at Birzeit University, joined him. Both of them would enter the graduate program in computer science.

In 2005, Fady, his wife Samar, and their infant daughter lost everything, including their home in the Lakeview neighborhood, in post-Katrina floods. Like so many New Orleanians, they sought refuge in Houston, Texas. It took them seventeen hours in terrible traffic to get there. It was traumatic. But Fady "put aside his own emotions" because he had an overwhelming desire to help others.

He volunteered to coordinate the Muslim American Society's Hurricane Katrina relief effort. Using his computer skills to match hundreds of Muslim volunteers and donations with the needs of evacuees, he first arranged for food to be taken to people at the George R. Brown Convention Center. Then he worked with others to develop a more comprehensive effort to assist with housing, counseling, health care, and schooling for children.

The experience changed him. "In 2005," he said, "I walked away from my master's and decided to dedicate my life to public service."

Helping people is hard work, and Fady Qaddoura was systematic in turning that [text continues at top of page 130].

In 2010, Fady Qaddoura was given the Senate Democrats' award for the intern who best exemplifies public service and the love of education. A decade later, he was elected to the Indiana Senate. *Credit: Senate Democrats.*

Rabia Jermoumi, Economist

Working as an economist in Indianapolis was not what Rabia Jermoumi expected to do.

Rabia Jermoumi grew up on a beach in Morocco. She still misses the ocean breeze, the leisurely walks in her bathing suit, the visits from extended family, and the long lunches in her parents' home, located just yards away from the Atlantic.

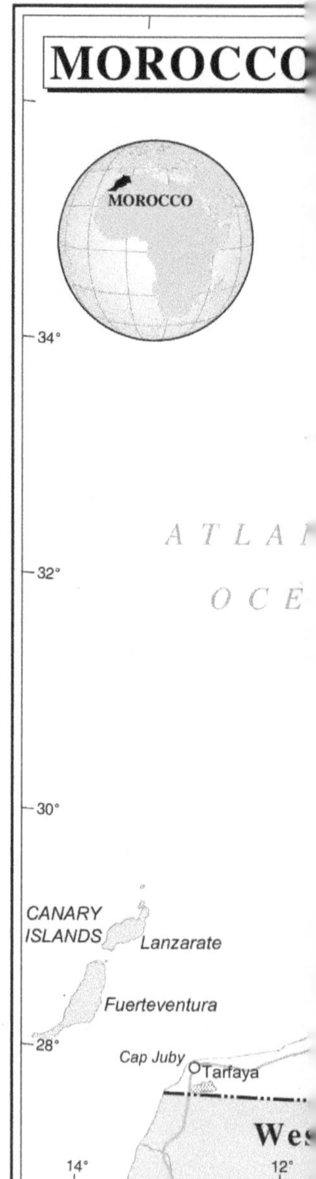

El Jadida is a port city of over 200,000 people that attracts lots of visitors during the summer. But it's a nice place to live anytime of the year: the average high temperature in August is around eighty-two degrees while the average low in January is forty-five degrees. The town is also home to a UNESCO World Heritage Site.

The daughter of a teacher and a bank director, both college educated, Rabia Jermoumi grew up speaking both Arabic and French, and she learned English in high school. "We had fun," she says, "but our parents made sure that education was our main focus." After secondary school, she enrolled in a six-year degree program at the Hassan II Institute for Agronomy and Veterinary Medicine, located in the city of Rabat.

In her final year, the University of Missouri invited her to do some research at their flagship campus. The plan was to spend the academic year in Missouri and then return to Morocco. Once she got there, her advisers were impressed. They encouraged her to apply for a PhD in agricultural economics. The university offered her financial support, and her parents were in favor. It took her about five years to finish. She wrote her dissertation on the economics of olive oil in the European Union.

Dr. Jermoumi had always planned on returning home. But love got in the way.

During her doctoral years, she married Mouhamad Alloosh, a physician and researcher from Jabadeen, Syria. They started a family. He took a position at IUPUI and brought their two children

Rabia Jermoumi grew up in the city of El Jadida, about seventy miles south of Casablanca. She went to university farther up the coast at Rabat. *Credit: United Nations.*

Rabia Jermoumi and a daughter stroll along the beach in Dr. Jermoumi's hometown, El Jadida. *Credit: Rabia Jermoumi.*

with him to Indianapolis so that Rabia could finish her dissertation. She joined them a year later.

Since then, Dr. Jermoumi has had a notable impact on health care and education in Indiana. Working as a health economist for the Regenstrief Institute, she used her expertise in econometrics to model how early intervention in patients with Alzheimer's disease would impact Medicare spending. The model showed that thorough intervention at the early stages of the disease—that is, spending more money at first—would actually "reduce or minimize healthcare expenditures" in the long run.

Rabia Jermoumi also spent eleven years working for the state of Indiana. She served as the research director and then chief information officer at the Indiana Commission of Higher Education (ICHE), which helps direct the mission of Indiana's public universities, approves new degree programs, and reviews public university budgets. Among the projects on which she worked at ICHE, she is proudest of the role she played in changing state policies about student financial aid.

Dr. Jermoumi studied the relationship between financial aid and student success in Indiana and other states. She developed models based on historical patterns that predicted how various policy changes in student aid might increase student retention and graduate rates. One of the problems ICHE hoped to solve was that too many students were running out of financial aid before finishing. They failed too

The Alloosh-Jermoumi kids give camel-riding a try in Marrakesh, Morocco. *Credit: Rabia Jermoumi.*

many classes and sometimes changed majors too often. Rabia Jermoumi's models predicted that student graduation rates would increase if students were required to enroll in a minimum number of credit hours per term and if they had to maintain a certain GPA. Though some disagreed with these mandates, student retention and graduation rates have increased in Indiana since they were implemented.

More recently, she teamed up with her husband and other scientists at a biomedical company called CorVus, where she serves as CFO and grant writer.

Rabia is also still busy raising her children. All four of them live at home, though one is now in college.

"My kids are just like any Americans whose parents come from a different country," she said. "They looked different, their names were different, and the food they took to school lunch was different." It did not surprise Rabia that "they struggled with that" because most children want to be seen as normal, to "be like everyone else."

Rabia and Mouhamad spoke to their children often—"I can't tell you how many nights we had the conversation"—about that reality. "Yes, we are different, we told them," Rabia said. "But let's take that difference as a way to empower you, to use that difference to be the best person you can be."

"It's a process they had to go through," Rabia believes. But the end result is anything but confusion.

"I am grateful that they are proud American Arab citizens now," Rabia says. "They say, 'we are Syrian Moroccan Americans.'" The children visit their extended families in both Morocco and Syria, although the 2011 Syrian civil war put a stop to the trips there. They understand but do not speak Arabic, at least not fluently yet. They identify with their families, their heritage, and their culture, especially the food.

Rabia's pride in her children goes beyond their identification with their Arab ethnicity. It also goes beyond their educational achievements. Rabia expresses deep joy about who they have become as human beings. "They are just great people," she exclaims.

She knows that they may face prejudice. Occasionally, people may stare at her headscarf or say something mean for no other reason than how she dresses. But Rabia is strong. She tells her kids that "I am not going to let them dictate who I am, what jobs I take, or what I do with my life." She will not allow fear to sabotage her dreams for herself, her children, or her community. "We are who we are," she says. "Find the courage within yourself to embrace it."

Does she still think about the beach? Oh, yes. "I miss everything," Rabia admits. "Growing up, I never thought that I would be living in the United States."

"But I'm thankful for it," she declared. "I mean, I always consider myself fortunate. I had the opportunity to come to this great country. I completed a PhD. I have a beautiful family. I have had good jobs."

Dr. Rabia Jermoumi's story counters the well-worn assumption that first-generation immigrants are inevitably torn between painful longing for their old country and devotion to their new one. Of course, there is always adjustment and sacrifice when we choose voluntarily to leave our hometown, wherever that is. But it is also possible that we can come to love more than one place. We can be part of more than one community. We can be Moroccan, Syrian, and American all at the same time.

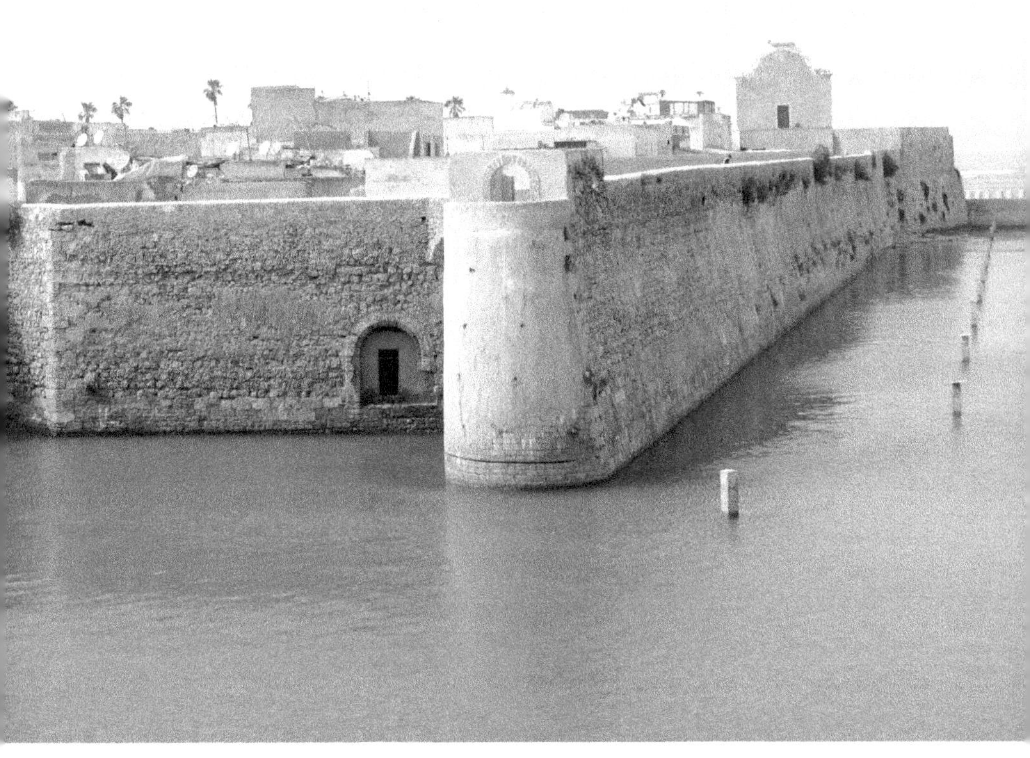

In 2004, UNESCO designated El Jadida a World Heritage Site. Among its many historic features are the massive fortress walls carved out of stone.

PROFILE: Educators Dounya Muslet and Nermeen Mouftah

Dounya Muslet, Elementary School Teacher

Dounya Muslet teaches fourth grade at Greenbriar Elementary School, located near the intersection of Eighty-Sixth Street and Ditch in the western part of Indianapolis's Washington Township. Most students at Greenbriar, which is known for embracing students from different backgrounds and abilities, qualify for a free or reduced lunch. A number of students speak languages other than English, including Spanish and Arabic. The majority of students are African American, but there are Latino/a, white, and international students too. In this interview, Miss Muslet—which is what her students call her—talks about why she became a teacher, the joys and the challenges of her profession, and her pride in her Palestinian heritage.

Q. Why did you become a teacher?

A. Growing up, all I ever wanted to do was be a mother. To be my mother. When people would ask, "What do you want to be when you get older?" I always used to say, "A mom." I remember being told once that I can't just be a mom, that I have to have a real job.

I wanted to be a teacher so that I could do what very few teachers did for me. I did not have a terrible upbringing. There were so many adults who loved me. But I faced a lot of childhood-based trauma. I wanted to make sure that every kid knows and feels that they are loved, and no matter what, that they have an adult who respects, understands, and supports them regardless of who they are, how they act, or where they come from.

Dounya Muslet with her *sitti*, or grandmother, Rahma Muslet. *Credit: Dounya Muslet.*

Being a teacher is so much more than teaching kids how to add and subtract. It's about being that adult that changes their life. Whether I am that person that they trust and confide in about things that no child should have to know or go through, or if I am just that role model that teaches them that it is okay to be weird or different and it's not "cool" to say bad words or to be mean to others. I wanted to make a difference.

Q. What is the best part and the most challenging part of your job?
A. The best part about my job is seeing the impact I have. The notes and drawings given to me by students. The complete 180-degree turn a student makes after having me as their teacher. The long-lasting relationships that continue beyond my class. The growth that we document using data that we collect throughout the year. If it weren't for these things, there is no way I could still be an educator.

The most challenging part about my job is a lot harder for me to identify. I guess if I have to say one thing, it would be the lack of respect and appreciation. Not necessarily from my school, students, or families, but from society. We are expected as educators to be this perfect person on social media, in school, and out in public; to know and teach everything from science to writing without making any mistakes; to teach children who really need a higher level of intervention but do not have an individualized education plan in place; and to create or buy materials to make learning more fun and engaging, no matter how many students we have. It feels like so few people really understand how underappreciated teachers are and why some teachers will never reach their full potential. We don't get paid enough, and we do not get the respect we deserve. It is by far the most challenging part of my job.

Q. What is special about Greenbriar?
A. Don't even get me started. Greenbriar was my dream school, but not for the reasons many would think. I had the opportunity as a junior at Ball State to visit an Indianapolis-based school where the daughter of my instructor, Dixie Denton, was teaching. I had never heard of Greenbriar but soon learned from my good friends, most of whom had graduated from North Central High School, that it was a Washington Township school that many of them had attended.

The first lesson I ever taught was in a kindergarten class at Greenbriar. I immediately felt everything that makes Greenbriar so special. The diversity. Greenbriar has one of the most diverse population of students I have ever seen. The people who work there. Not just the teachers. I am talking about

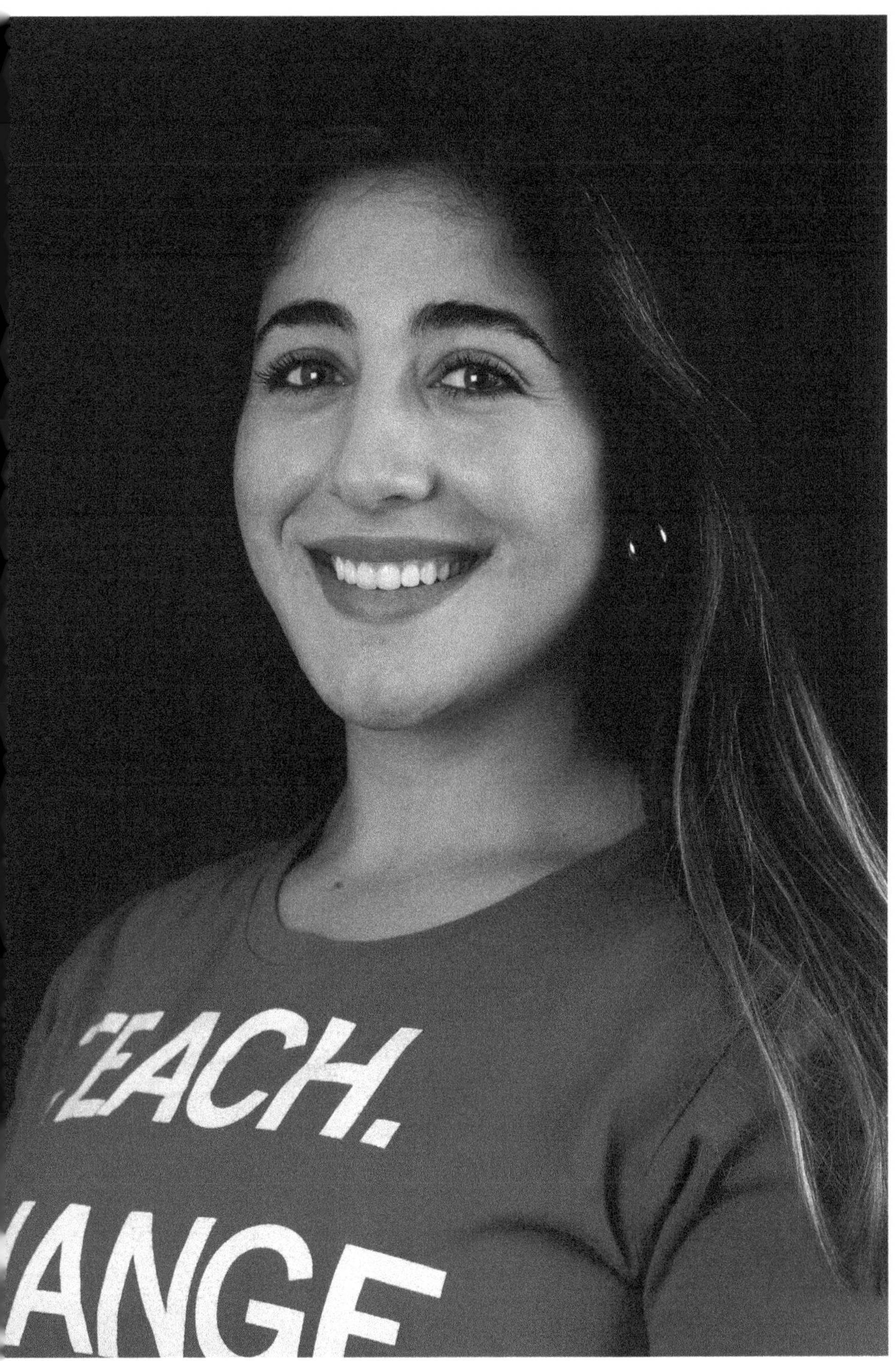

Dounya Muslet. *Credit: Ziad Hefni.*

everyone from the front office staff to the custodial staff. Every adult in that building is dedicated to the success of all its students. We all support one another. I can't imagine working anywhere else.

Q. What does your Arab heritage mean to you?
A. Both of my parents are of Palestinian descent. Growing up, I was sometimes told by my grandmother to lie about where we were from. To say I was Jordanian and not Palestinian. As an adult, I was not only ashamed but sad that anyone, especially my family, would be embarrassed or scared of telling others the truth.

I am a very proud Palestinian. Being of Palestinian heritage is one of the most meaningful things to and about me. Not because I can speak the language, because I can't, or even because I was raised so deep in the culture. Being a Palestinian makes me proud and sets me apart from others because it is a reminder of my people who fought and continue to fight for what is theirs and what they want. I feel like it means so much to me because as a little kid I learned so much about my heritage, and then it was sort of taken away after my parents divorced and I moved away. My learning stopped for a while. I was (and still am) often teased for being so "white" or Americanized. For a short time, I acted as if I was happier that way, and I adopted American society's preconceived notions about what it means to be Palestinian. But it did not take long for me to realize that I had a huge hole within me that craved my culture and religion. I am constantly doing what I can to be a better Palestinian because I don't want my future children to ever be ashamed of where their family is from, the language they speak, or the clothes they wear.

Q. What would you like your legacy to be?
A. My hope is that long after I am gone, those who knew me are kinder and more empathetic toward others than they were before knowing me. I would like to be remembered for the kindness I showed toward others. Most importantly, I want others to love one another. Love each other no matter what, and make sure they show their love through actions and not just words. I want to be remembered as a teacher. To be remembered for teaching my students to believe in themselves no matter what, because they are capable of so much more than they ever could have imagined.

Nermeen Mouftah, Professor

Nermeen Mouftah, PhD, is an assistant professor specializing in Islam and the anthropology of religion at Butler University. She's Canadian, but her parents are from Alexandria, Egypt. In this interview, she discusses her research and teaching and reflects on why she chose to become a professor.

Q. Where did you grow up?
A. I was born and raised in Kingston, Ontario. It's a small city of about 100,000 people. In Canada, it's known to be a city of prisons and universities. It was the country's first capital city, so the downtown has some beautiful old architecture. It's on Lake Ontario. My parents are Alexandrians, so the water was always something we appreciated.

Q. How and why did you come to Indianapolis?
A. I moved to Indianapolis to take up a position at Butler University.

Q. What is your education?
A. I studied political science and literature for my BA at the University of Toronto. I went on to study for an MA in literature at University College London. I took a break from graduate school for a few years, first to teach and then later to work in international development. I took on an internship that led me to Cairo to work for the International Labor Organization. While in Egypt, I went back to school and did a graduate diploma in Islamic studies at the American University in Cairo. I fell in love with my subjects there, and that led me back to the University of Toronto for my doctoral training.

Q. What classes do you teach? What are the most important lessons you teach?
A. The courses I most frequently teach are the general introduction to Islam; Islam, Gender, and Sexuality; and Modern Middle East and North Africa. I also teach a course on the intersections of religion, politics, and economy called Moral Economies: Religion, Politics, and the Marketplace. I offer a first-year seminar on questions of development, humanitarianism, and social inequality called Doing Good in the World: Human Responses to Social Inequality. This coming semester, I will teach Religions of the World for the first time. In the past, I have taught Qur'an as well as Islam in America and look forward to returning to those topics soon.

Q. What research do you do?
A. I'm interested in how Muslims grapple with questions of progress, care, and

Nermeen Mouftah. *Credit: Ziad Hefni.*

justice. I come at my questions anthropologically. That means I'm interested in what people do, which leads me to spend plenty of time observing my research subjects (what anthropologists call "participant-observation") as well as conducting interviews, among other research practices. I write about how religious authorities, activists, and everyday people articulate "Islamic solutions" to problems of poverty and exclusion, and I examine the sometimes contradictory effects of their efforts. Currently, I'm at work on two projects. In the first, I'm completing a book manuscript titled *Read in the Name of Your Lord: Islamic Literacy Activism between Reform and Revolution*. It looks at the role of activism for basic literacy in Egypt's January 25 uprising as it intersected with religious revival. The second project, *Guardians of Faith: Orphans and the Remaking of the Muslim Family*, asks how Islam shapes the legal, biological, and emotional negotiations involved in the care and abandonment of vulnerable children. This research led me to research in the US, Morocco, and Pakistan.

Q. What are the challenges and joys of being an Arab American professor in Indianapolis?

A. As far as I am aware, I am the only Arab professor in my college. That identity, along with being Canadian, and certainly the particularity of my academic training, mean that I often feel I can contribute a fresh perspective to the conversation. That is certainly a joy, but it can sometimes be a burden.

Similarly, in the classroom, I often introduce students to their first exposure to Islam, Muslims, Arabs, and the Middle East beyond Hollywood depictions or news headlines. I take that task seriously since I have seen it be transformative. The challenge is in treating our topics with the same complexity and nuance that students can allow for subjects more familiar to them.

Q. Why did you become a professor? Is it what you expected? Why or why not?

A. Ultimately, I think I became a professor because it was a job that allowed me to do my favorite things: reading, writing, and teaching. When I started my PhD, I don't think I would have thought of it that way, but looking back, that's what stands out. As I started my PhD, I did not yet think of academia as a career choice so much as I thought of it as the path I had to take to (at least in a socially acceptable way) dedicate my time to thinking, study, and writing.

An academic life was something of a natural decision for me. I grew up in a university town where my father taught in the engineering department. At the time, Kingston didn't have a mosque, so the Muslim community (a tight-knit and genuinely loving community) held all of their events on campus, from Friday prayers to potluck dinners. So between that and spending weekend afternoons at my dad's office, the university campus was an exciting and nourishing place for me.

I am glad that I spent a few years in my twenties pursuing other jobs. I think that helped me decisively choose academia. The balance between researching, writing, and teaching is what makes the life of a professor so attractive to me. I love the ability I have in my work to be creative, and the space and time I have to teach courses and dedicate myself to projects that are meaningful to me. I'm genuinely grateful almost every day.

CHAPTER FIVE

THE CULINARY CONTRIBUTION

Arab Americans are not the only ethnic group in Indianapolis whose community life often revolves around food, but the preparation and consumption of dishes from North Africa and the Middle East is especially important in Arab Indianapolis. Parents do not always pass on the Arabic language or even their religion to their children, but there is almost always someone in a family who preserves granny's recipes. Holidays aren't the same without that food or the arguments that sometimes erupt over the right way to prepare it. Arab foods evoke not only the places from which Arab Americans have come, but also the importance of Arab family and community in Indianapolis. As Helen Corey's story illustrates, it has also become a passport to public recognition for Arab culture. By sharing this culinary heritage with others outside the home, Arab Americans turn Indianapolis into a space where something that was once foreign becomes an everyday aspect of Hoosier culture.

Holidays / Holy Days

Not all Arab Hoosiers, like Hoosiers more generally, are religious, but most Arab Americans trace their roots to Christianity or Islam—and most of them observe major religious holidays of some sort. Perhaps the most popular holiday is Christmas—in addition to all the Christians who participate in the holiday, some secular Arab Americans, Muslims, and Jews celebrate it, not so much for religious reasons but because Santa, Christmas trees, gift giving, and even Christmas music loom large in American culture. The major Arab American Christian holidays are Christmas and Easter, which celebrate, respectively, the birth of Jesus and his resurrection three days after his death. The most important Arab American Muslim holidays are Eid al-Fitr, which marks the end of the sacred month of fasting, and Eid al-Adha, which is observed at the end of the annual pilgrimage to Mecca.

Even if Arab Americans celebrate different religious holidays, they often serve the same Arab foods during these events. For example, Arab Americans who trace their roots to the Eastern Mediterranean, like the George and Shatara families, share the same culinary heritage. Food has always been central to Arab American culture, and Arabic-speaking immigrants and their heirs make a special effort to prepare the dishes most associated with the region or country to which they trace their roots. Such traditions are often inseparable from the celebration of the holiday itself. These foods nourish not only our bodies but also the memories and the love we share with friends and family members who value Arab American community and identity. In the following two sections, two Arab Americans, Steve George and Amnah Shatara, describe in their own words the important role Arab food plays during various holiday traditions.

Christmas, as told by Steve George

My dad was one of six kids, and his parents immigrated from the Middle East in 1906. He was born in 1908. My mom learned to make a lot of Arab food, and around Christmas time, we would do kibbeh saniyeh—a baked meat dish with fine ground beef and bulgur wheat that's layered in a three-inch high pan with onions, pine nuts, and coarse ground meat in the middle. Then you put another layer of the bulgur wheat and fine ground beef. It's typically baked and browned with quite a bit of butter. Green beans and rice were also served around the holidays.

We would sometimes have fatayer, or meat pies—coarse ground meat and onions, sometimes with pine nuts, rolled into a triangular shaped pie and then baked. The other two dishes that we would make frequently were cabbage rolls and grape leaves. And then for the grape leaves and kibbeh there would always be laban, which is yogurt, and typically it's homemade yogurt.

We made desserts too, especially baklava. My aunt, Ruth Khoury George, was known for making ma'amoul—a shortbread cookie but a little more crisp, covered in powdered sugar. She would make something called ka'ik, sort of a pretzel looking thing that had rosewater flavoring. It was kind of sweet, but very dense.

When we were kids, we would always have a Christmas play at St. George Church, and we would play various parts like Mary, Joseph, the three wise men—kind of a nativity play.

When I was young, you wore your Sundays best to go to church. The ladies were always in dresses, and when I was growing up, they covered their hair—I wouldn't call it a bonnet but almost like a laced doily. Men were always in suits and ties. As a boy I would have to wear coat and tie on the holidays; outside the holidays it was dress slacks, a shirt, and sometimes a tie too.

As my kids were growing up, we used the Orthodox prayer book—a pocket prayer book—during the holidays and the rest of the year too. All the prayers run on an annual cycle. Our prayers and our chants reflect the seasonal message.

Previous page: Both the George and Shatara families traditionally eat fatayer, or pies, during the holidays. They can be stuffed with meat, cheese, or spinach. *Credit: Amnah Shatara.*

Top: Steve George's extended family not only gathered for holidays but also every Sunday at the house of his aunt, Ruth George. *Credit: Steve George, St. George Church.*

Bottom: The 1976 Children's Christmas Play at St. George Church featured angels and shepherds. *Credit: Faris Mesalam, St. George Church.*

Right: Shortbread cookies stuffed with dates, figs, or other fruits are popular throughout the Arab Middle East. *Credit: Amnah Shatara.*

Eid al-Fitr, as told by Amnah Shatara

About a week before Eid al-Fitr comes, we get prepared. We prepare sweets and special foods, and we shop for new clothes. It's a tradition to buy new clothes. And then comes the new moon sighting.

We get up the morning of Eid and you dress up, you put on cologne, and you get real fancy. And then we drive either to the masjid—to the mosque—or because there are so many Muslims who want to pray, we use a school gym. One year, we went to the Grand Park in Westfield.

Everybody likes to wear their country's clothing. I don't want to brag, but this is the truth: when I moved to Indy in 1991, I would go to the activities we have at the masjid, and my husband said, "We're Palestinian, why don't you wear the Palestinian traditional clothes? When are you going to wear it?" And I'm like, "Oh, that's a good idea." So I would wear mine, and people from Pakistan, India, and Ghana—they always wear theirs.

We spend the first day of Eid—it's three days total—on the phone calling people we haven't spoken to in years or months. You call your relatives. During Ramadan, the night before, some people may have little grudges or something, and you should call them and ask for forgiveness. We'll call the family first, especially the elderlies—we have to start with the elderlies. I have two older sisters, so I will call them, and then my mother-in-law and uncles. We send cards, we do FaceTime, we Zoom.

And then we just eat, eat, eat, eat for three days! A lot of people try to take some days off from work, and if you can't, that's still okay.

We buy kids gifts. Back home, they would give them money. But here, with Christmas, you know the kids kind of feel like, "Well, why do we just get money?" So now, we do give them money—my husband always gives them money—but I say, I don't care, I'm gonna go buy them some toys too.

Amnah and Taiseer Shatara enjoy spending Eid al-Fitr with their grandchildren. *Credit: Taiseer Shatara.*

There are certain prayers we do, like, "God is forgiving, he is merciful, he forgives, please forgive me." We have to repeat this a lot during Ramadan. We believe that the doors of hell are shut, okay? And the doors of heaven are open. So you should do a lot of prayers, ask God for forgiveness, ask God Almighty for His mercy to purify us, to help us. And, you know, you can do anything for thirty days, but you're hoping that you can carry, if not all, then some of it throughout the year. Until the next Ramadan.

Maqluba (Upside Down)

There is no better example of Palestinian home cooking than this one-pot meat and rice dish which can be flipped upside down in dramatic fashion when served. Cooks generally use chicken or lamb, but a vegan version of the dish can be made with chickpeas. A healthier version of the dish also avoids frying the eggplant and cauliflower, instead roasting them until slightly browned in the oven.

1 cauliflower and/or 1 eggplant
2 onions
2 pounds lamb pieces (from the leg, preferably) or 1 whole chicken, cut up
1 teaspoon ground allspice
1 teaspoon cinnamon
2 cups basmati rice
1/3 cup pine nuts or slivered almonds
Vegetable or olive oil

Cook the meat. Combine the lamb or chicken in a five-quart Dutch oven or other pot with two sliced onions, cinnamon, allspice, pepper, and one teaspoon or more of salt, to taste. If desired, you can also add a crushed clove of garlic, a bay leaf, three cloves, and/or three green cardamom pods. Cover with about six cups of water, bring to a boil, and then reduce to a simmer. Cook until the meat is tender, as much as one hour. When done, remove the meat, drain the broth into a separate container, and dispose of the onion and spices.

Cook the vegetables. While the meat is cooking, partially peel the eggplant, slice it into one-inch-thick rounds, and then cut into half-moons. Season with a teaspoon of salt and set in a colander for a half hour. The eggplant will sweat, and then you should wipe off as much of the salt as you can. You can also skip the eggplant and use only cauliflower. If you like, substitute or add carrot (sliced into two-inch chunks) and a sliced potato. You should end up with about two pounds of vegetables. Fry the vegetables in oil until they are golden brown or coat them with some oil and roast them in the oven at 350 degrees until slightly brown. Sprinkle them with salt, if desired.

Assemble the pot. Place the cooked meat on the bottom of the pan, then put the vegetables on top. Add two cups of rinsed and drained rice, one teaspoon of salt, and three cups of the reserved broth.

Cook the pot. Now you have a decision to make. Cook it on the stove, using low enough heat so that the bottom of the pot does not burn, or take the easier route of cooking it for thirty minutes to an hour in a 350-degree oven. Test the rice to see if it is done. If too dry, add some more broth and let it cook a few minutes more until the liquid is absorbed.

Now for the fun. You might want another pair of hands for this step. Place a large platter over the top of the pot. Make sure you use an oven mitt or pot holder as you flip the pot upside down onto the platter. (If it ends up a mess, no worries. It will still taste good.) Let the pot rest on top of the platter for at least five minutes before removing.

Garnish and serve. Toast the pine nuts or almonds in olive oil or butter until slightly brown, and then use them to garnish the maqluba. Serve with yogurt on the side.

Arab Restaurants

Arab Americans in Indianapolis have been serving food to the public for decades—from the "Oriental" dinners offered at the Syrian American Brotherhood clubhouse and St. George Syrian Orthodox Church in the 1930s to the monthly "Arabian Nights" at Mike Tamer Jr.'s Steak Haus on College Avenue in the 1960s. Almost all of that food was based on family recipes from Syria, Lebanon, and Palestine. But after US immigration policy changed in 1965, immigrants began to arrive from across North Africa and the Middle East, and after a while, the Arab food scene in Indianapolis became more diverse. There are now many Arab-owned restaurants that serve some kind of Arab food in Indianapolis. A number of these sell Greek-style gyro sandwiches or falafels, balls of garbanzo bean flour and Mediterranean spices fried in oil and topped with salad and tahini sauce, made out of sesame seed paste and lemon juice. A few, like Al-Basha in Fishers, are both a restaurant and a market, offering all the ingredients and brands that are sometimes hard to find in conventional stores. The shelves of Al-Basha are stocked with imported olives, sesame seed paste, pickles, bulgur, lentils, date cookies, and spices such as sumac and thyme. Its refrigerator cases contain various Middle Eastern cheeses, yogurt, and meats. The market also offers freshly baked flatbread.

While many Arab restaurants are now well established, anyone who has owned a restaurant will tell you that it's hard to make it in the business. Ms. Nabila, the Jordanian chef at Sahara Restaurant in Broad Ripple, says that she and her husband tried to follow the script for a successful restaurant. In 2016, they rented space right on Broad Ripple Avenue, a high traffic area. They paid a lot of money to a marketing agency. They hired experienced managers. But for the most part, their

Eid al-Fitr at the Shatara house features warak inab, or stuffed grape leaves; musakhkhan, chicken with onion and sumac; and maqluba, or upside-down, among other dishes. *Credit: Amnah Shatara.*

SAHARA
GYROS &
AUTHENTIC MEDITERRANEAN FOOD!!
OPEN
SHAWARMA
GYRO
SAHARA
GYROS & WINGS
HOURS
SUNDAY TO THURSDAY
FRI & SAT

The booths inside Sahara Restaurant, located in Broad Ripple, are separated by mashrabiya latticework, which is traditionally used in the Arab world to screen balconies and windows. *Credit: Edward Curtis.*

SAFFRON CAFE

Housed in a brick building in downtown Indianapolis, Saffron Café's interior and exterior are designed colorfully to play with Moroccan and other Arab images and architectural elements to distinguish itself from its surroundings. *Credit: Edward Curtis.*

Rayyan is one of dozens of international restaurants and shops at Lafayette and Thirty-Eighth Street in Indianapolis. *Credit: Edward Curtis.*

hopes for success have been unfulfilled. Many of the young customers who frequent bars in the area want to drink alcohol, which they do not serve. Their marketing consultants did not do a good job. There aren't many Arabs who live in Broad Ripple. Though Sahara Café serves hard-to-find mansaf, the Jordanian national dish of stewed lamb served with salty yogurt sauce, its menu is composed mainly of the sandwiches, hummus, and salads that one can find in at least two other restaurants in Broad Ripple. It's a competitive environment, but Ms. Nabila, also known as Umm Hamza, hopes that over time, more people will find their way to her restaurant.

Olive oil, parsley, chickpeas, lamb, and yogurt are common elements in the cuisines served across North Africa and the Middle East, but there is no one kind of Arab food. Arab cuisines reflect the multiple cultural influences of the empires that have ruled in the region, the traders who have traveled through it, the recipes shared along the Silk Road and across the Sahara, and the many ethnic-religious groups that have lived in the Arabic-speaking world.

There is no better local teacher on the diverse influences of Arab cuisine than chef Anass Sentissi, the owner of Saffron Café in downtown Indianapolis. He points out that Moroccan food shows the impact not only of Morocco's indigenous Imazighen (or Berbers) but also of Arabs, sub-Saharan Africans, the

Indianapolis artist Joanie Youngman made this painting of Canal Bistro as a gift to owners George, who is from Egypt, and Mona, who is from Lebanon. *Credit: Joanie Youngman.*

Spanish, the French, and others. Chef Sentissi is himself a culmination of many influences and interests. He is a percussionist who majored in ethnomusicology at Indiana University, Bloomington; he loves to play the music of Andalusia. He restores old homes to their former splendor, including a twenty-two-room house in historic Woodruff Place. Sentissi grew up in Morocco with seven brothers and two sisters, and he stuck close to his mother in the kitchen, where he helped cook for the entire family. He worked at a family restaurant in Bloomington and then opened his own in Indianapolis in 2009.

With colorful decor and a lively facade, Saffron Café made an immediate splash. It didn't hurt that the restaurant offered live music in the evenings—sometimes featuring the oud, or Middle Eastern lute. There was belly dancing too. But the star has always been the food. The restaurant offered honeyed Cornish hen, fish kebab, lamb tagine, paella, and harira, the Moroccan national soup. His signature scent was saffron, the most expensive spice in the world, as he enjoyed pointing out. Chef Sentissi also offered cooking classes in the restaurant's small kitchen. He eventually published his own cookbook. *Saffron for All Seasons: Holistic Recipes for Optimum Health and Jubilant Wellness* (2019) quotes Hippocrates and Avicenna (Ibn Sina) in making its case for a holistic approach to diet. Among the book's major topics

Al Basha restaurant in Fishers, Indiana, starts out as a regular café, but then as you step into the dining room, it evokes the feeling of a Palestinian home. *Credit: Ziad Hefni.*

are whole grains, the glycemic index, and bio-identifiable theory. The book includes recipes for many of the dishes served in his Indianapolis restaurant. Reading the book, it becomes clear why Chef Rantissi has been able to please so many diners for over a decade. His food embodies the many sides of the man himself: philosopher, musician, historian, healer, and host.

A different kind of Arab restaurant can be found in the Rayyan Restaurant and Bakery, which prepares the cuisine of a country over 3,500 miles to the east of Morocco. It serves the food of Yemen. Its founder, Abdulwahab Albashaar, is from Ibb, a town in the southwestern part of the country with a population of over 150,000. After immigrating to the Detroit area and then to Indianapolis, Albashaar, a school principal by trade, opened the doors of the restaurant in 2015. His son, Muhammad, became the manager, often appearing on social media to promote the restaurant's brand.

Located in a strip mall on Thirty-Eighth Street near Lafayette Square, the restaurant has a large, red sign that glows at night, greeting diners in both English and Arabic. Huge photographs of its signature dishes are featured on the restaurant's windows. The look of it evokes, for lack of a better term, an authentic Arab restaurant where regular people, rather than tourists, would eat in the old country. Rayyan prepares what is called zabiha meat, meaning that the animal has been butchered according to Islamic religious guidelines. Muslims can purchase carry-out dinners during the Islamic month of Ramadan in which believers break their fasts after the sun goes down each day.

Rayyan has a large menu, but what is special are the Yemeni dishes. There is lamb hanidh, which is coated with a mixture of olive oil, green onions, garlic, chives and spices such as cumin, black pepper, turmeric, coriander, cardamom, and cinnamon, and then slow roasted. You can buy one plate of it, or you can buy the whole lamb. Chicken Mandi is also available. It is topped with a rich spice paste that included garlic and ginger and then roasted, traditionally in a clay pot. There is also saltah, the Yemeni national stew, a flexible dish that includes broth, meat, and root vegetables but whose one essential ingredient is hilbeh, or Fenugreek froth. Most Yemenis eat it with bread.

There is little doubt when you are at Rayyan that you are in an Arab restaurant. But not all eateries that serve Arab food are exclusively or even explicitly Arab. Many restauranteurs prefer to offer a wider menu of Mediterranean food, including Greek, Turkish, and other dishes. For example, Canal Bistro in Broad Ripple, where customers can sit indoors or on a patio along a canal, focuses on Syrian-Lebanese dishes popular throughout the world: hummus, or chickpea dip; tabbouli, or parsley salad; shawarma, or sliced meat cooked on a spit; kafta kabab, or grilled meatballs; lamb kebab;

and fattoush, salad with fried pita. They also serve Greek gyros; spanakopita, or spinach pies; and moussaka, or eggplant casserole. There is an American-style brunch on the weekends. Having a diverse menu is no betrayal of Middle Eastern culinary culture. Today, one can find all these foods in the eastern Mediterranean, and many Arab people enjoy consuming them too. Arab tastes keep changing. Diets incorporate new ingredients and styles of cooking. Arab cooking has always been dynamic.

The most important thing about this cuisine, besides its nutritional value of course, is that it brings people together. It is one of the most tangible Arab contributions to the city, changing what people eat, experience, and enjoy. There are now many places, from simple sandwich places to fancier sit-down restaurants, where people in Indianapolis can consume this delicious food. It is one of the more popular examples of how Arabs and their cultures have become part of Indianapolis. Food is the most public face of cultural encounter. Arab-owned restaurants provide the space where Arabs and non-Arabs, cooks and customers, can meet one another, strike up a conversation, and create the feeling that this city is big enough for all of its people, a city that finds delight in its differences.

Meditation on Helen Corey's Tabbouli

Wheat Garden Salad
1 cup cracked wheat, fine
1 bunch green onions
2 large bunches parsley
1/2 bunch mint
4 large tomatoes
Juice of 4 lemons
1/2 cup olive oil
Salt and pepper to taste

Soak wheat in water a few minutes. Squeeze dry by pressing between palms. Chop onions, parsley, mint leaves, and tomatoes very fine. Add wheat, lemon juice, olive oil, salt, and pepper. Mix well. Serve with fresh lettuce leaves, grape leaves, or cabbage leaves used as scoops. Serves six.

Tabbouli, originally from Syria and Lebanon, is now a popular dish around the world. Helen Corey's 1962 recipe for the dish, which she also calls "suf," is, like most of her recipes, concise. Its economical prose conceals the

sometimes spirited arguments that Arab Indianapolis cooks have about the best way to prepare it. For example, some people add cucumber and even a little radish to the dish. Others omit the black pepper, saying it ruins the taste of the salad. Corey's inclusion of four lemons, one half bunch of mint, and an entire bunch of onions means hers is a strong, even aggressive tabbouli—there are no subtle hints of this or that. Most importantly, Helen Corey's recipe dares not to broach the solemn question of the proper ratio of bulgur wheat to parsley. But she tips her hand in giving tabbouli the English name, "wheat garden salad."

"Wheat salad?!" a hundred other cooks might exclaim. "No, this is a *parsley* salad."

In the past, adding more wheat may have signaled the wealth of the household in which the tabbouli was made. Wheat used to be more expensive than parsley. But Arab restaurants and chefs in the Middle East have long since settled this question in favor of more parsley, less wheat. One standard tabbouli recipe, for example, calls for one quarter cup of cracked wheat and two bunches of parsley. That is, it recommends using one fourth of the amount of wheat that Helen Corey's recipe demands.

Helen Corey's tabbouli reflected the practice of many Arab American families who preferred a wheatier version. But the emphasis on wheat went too far when, in the late twentieth century, instant tabbouli appeared as a shelf-stable item in US grocery stores and was offered on US salad bars. There is nothing wrong with a wheat salad. But it was offensive when manufacturers dressed it with a smattering of freeze-dried parsley and mint and an overwhelming amount of citric acid. The proliferation of Arab restaurants in Indianapolis has thankfully addressed this problem by offering actual tabbouli to the public.

Whatever quibbles another member of the Arab Indianapolis community may have with Helen Corey's formula for what she labels "the most popular of all Arabic salads," there is one sentence in her recipe that evokes meanings so deep that they compel tears in their repeating. *Squeeze dry by pressing between palms.* It likely sounds technical and devoid of affect to those who did not spend time with their Arab American grandmothers, uncles, and other relatives in the kitchen. But for those of us who were there to see it, the careful and methodical squeezing of water-swollen wheat by the hands of someone who cooked for you because they loved you is a memory that makes us beyond grateful for having been born Arab.

Left: As a child, the author was taught to use a lot of bulgur wheat when making tabbouli. After living in the Middle East, however, his version came to favor parsley. *Credit: Edward Curtis.*

ACKNOWLEDGMENTS

As I learned about the long history of Arabic-speaking people in Indianapolis, I felt like I was meeting members of my own family for the first time. I trace my own Arab roots to the Hamaway, Saffa, and Samaha families from Syria and Lebanon. Like many of the people in this book, they first immigrated to the United States before World War I. My granny helped to raise me as a proud Arab, and she taught me about many of the stories and traditions that I saw reflected in the history of Arab Indianapolis—from the stuffed grape leaves to the hope that Palestinians will one day be free. But there were also surprises at every turn. The story of Arab Indianapolis ended up being richer than anything I had imagined. There are a lot of books and articles on Arab Americans in the United States, but Indianapolis barely warrants a mention in any of them. There are also lots of books and articles about Indianapolis—but Arabic-speaking people do not figure prominently in them. This book of photographs is a step forward in recognizing the legacy of Arab Indianapolis. Until people like Helen Corey and Fady Qaddoura—just to name two people—become household names in Indiana, we have work to do, not just for ourselves, but for our whole community. Indianapolis is sometimes stereotyped as a sleepy, white-bread town. We have always been more cosmopolitan than that.

I first proposed the idea for the Arab Indianapolis project to the Indiana Muslim Advocacy Network, Catholic Charities' Indianapolis and Refugee Services, and Eman Schools, all of whom agreed to partner with IUPUI to bring these stories to light. Deacon Joseph Olas and Father Anthony Yazge of St. George Antiochian Orthodox Church were also essential to the project's success. Some of this book's best photographs are from the church's collection. A little later, Indianapolis Public Library's Stephen Lane volunteered to help, and the library has been a wonderful resource. My colleague, Professor Jeff Wilson, also partnered with me and designed two fantastic maps of Syrian grocers for the book.

So many community members were supportive. First, there were all the people who were interviewed and quoted for this book. Many of them connected me with other Arab Americans. In addition, a number of people gave me advice about the project, especially Hiba Alami, Samia Alajlouni, Mohammad Al-Haddad, and Eyas Raddad. Josh Chitwood, a descendant of Abraham Freije, was generous with photographs, information, and encouragement. Three of Helen Corey's nieces—Cathy Azar, Sandy Kassis, and Char Wade—provided invaluable assistance. Thanks, as well, to Joan Bey, Matt Holdzkom, Father Paul Fuller, Nadia Kousari, and Julie Slaymaker.

The sources used for this book include US census records, ship manifests, military records, birth and death certificates, and marriage licenses, all available through Ancestry.com, city directories, Sanborn Insurance maps and Baist atlases, newspapers, and interviews. I assembled a team of IUPUI student researchers to help me explore these sources. We sought to discover where Indianapolis's Arabic-speaking immigrants came from and how they got here. The insurance maps and city directories then helped us figure out where they lived and what those places looked like. Professor Paul Mullins taught me how to use these sources effectively, and then I passed that know-how on to students. We also used keyword searches in Indianapolis newspapers and conducted interviews. Jay Brodzeller and Ronnie Kawak worked on the project from the beginning, and then Dana Dobbins, Lily Malcomb, and Jamee West signed on. Asrar Jaber interviewed a couple restaurant owners for me. IUPUI Honors students Emma Eldridge, Layla Mitiche, and Mickey Yoder also made important contributions. It was a lot more fun to work in collaboration with students on this project, and I so appreciate their willingness to join me on this intellectual adventure.

I was also fortunate to find Ziad Hefni, a photographer and member of the local Arab American community who also happens to be an IUPUI student. His photographs are featured throughout this book, which would not have taken shape without his hard work. Ziad, who traces his roots to Egypt and Syria, attended Eman High School, a Muslim school in Fishers, Indiana.

Dan Crissman, my editor, made this a much better book, and it was a pleasure to work with the entire team at Belt Publishing.

Every effort has been made to identify all those who hold the rights to the photographs included in this book. The publishers would be pleased to hear from any rights holders who have not been properly recognized.

Funding for *Arab Indianapolis* was provided through the endowed professorship that I hold, the William M. and Gail M. Plater Chair of the Liberal Arts at IUPUI. I am grateful for the opportunity it has given me to do such meaningful labor.

Page 170: Edward Curtis. *Credit: Ziad Hefni.*

CPSIA information can be obtained
at www.ICGtesting.com
Printed in the USA
JSHW010811120322
23797JS00001B/1